Charles Darwin

And the Evolution Revolution

Owen Gingerich
General Editor

Charles Darwin

And the Evolution Revolution

Rebecca Stefoff

Oxford University Press
New York • Oxford

To my mother, with love

Oxford University Press

Oxford New York
Athens Auckland Bangkok Bombay
Calcutta Cape Town Dar es Salaam Delhi
Florence Hong Kong Istanbul Karachi
Kuala Lumpur Madras Madrid Melbourne
Mexico City Nairobi Paris Singapore
Taipei Tokyo Toronto Warsaw
and associated companies in
Berlin Ibadan

Copyright © 1996 by Rebecca Stefoff
Published by Oxford University Press, Inc.,
198 Madison Avenue, New York, New York 10016
First issued as an Oxford University Press paperback in 1998

Oxford is a registered trademark of Oxford University Press

Design: Design Oasis
Layout: Leonard Levitsky
Picture research: Patricia Burns

Library of Congress Cataloging-in-Publication Data
Charles Darwin and the evolution revolution / Stefoff, Rebecca
p. cm. — (Oxford portraits in science)
Includes bibliographical references and index.
ISBN 0-19-508996-0 (library edition); ISBN 0-19-512028-0 (paperback)
1. Darwin, Charles, 1809–1882—Juvenile literature.
2. Naturalists—England—Biography—Juvenile literature.
[1. Darwin, Charles, 1809–1882. 2. Naturalists.]
I. Title. II. Series.
QH31.D2S82   1996
575'.0092—dc20   95-35802
[B]   CIP

9 8 7 6 5

Printed in the United States of America
on acid-free paper

On the cover: *Charles Darwin in 1881, the year before his death.* Inset: *Darwin in 1851.*
Frontispiece: *Darwin photographed on the veranda at Down House, 1881.*

Contents

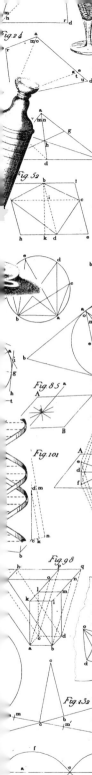

OXFORD PORTRAITS in SCIENCE

Charles Darwin sat for this portrait in 1840, a few years after his round-the-world voyage in the Beagle. His expression is placid, but the ideas forming behind that broad brow would eventually send shock waves through Victorian society.

Starting Points

On September 15, 1835, a small ship called the *Beagle* sailed toward a cluster of islands that lie scattered across the equator in the Pacific Ocean, some 600 miles off the west coast of South America. Aboard the *Beagle* a young scientist named Charles Darwin eagerly awaited a glimpse of land. The first island he saw, however, was a disappointment. "Nothing could be less inviting than the first appearance," he wrote in his journal. The landscape was a broken field of black lava, rising in rugged peaks that were gouged by deep, gaping crevasses. A few stunted, leafless bushes were the only signs of life. Robert FitzRoy, the *Beagle*'s captain, compared the hot, desolate island to hell, and Darwin wrote, "The dry and parched surface, being heated by the noonday sun, gave to the air a close and sultry feeling, like that from a stove: we fancied even that the bushes smelt unpleasantly." This was Darwin's introduction to the Galápagos Islands. Dismal and lifeless as they seemed at first, these islands were to play a vital role in Darwin's work— work that would revolutionize humankind's understanding of life on this planet.

The British government had sent the *Beagle* and its crew on a round-the-world expedition aimed at improving the sailing charts used by the navy. Robert FitzRoy, captain of the *Beagle*, had been assigned to survey many coasts and harbors, including those of the remote, isolated Galápagos Islands. Yet a different kind of survey of the Galápagos—an unofficial one, made by the 26-year-old Darwin—eventually overshadowed all of FitzRoy's careful measurements.

Darwin's passion was natural history, the study of the earth and all the living things upon it. While FitzRoy and the other officers diligently mapped the Galápagos, Darwin studied the plants and animals that lived on the islands. Many of the specimens he observed or collected were new to science. Indeed, the only Galápagos creature that was well known to naturalists was the giant tortoise.

Sixteenth-century Spanish seafarers had named the islands for these huge, slow-moving tortoises (*galápago* is Spanish for tortoise); later the creatures were carried away by the tens of thousands to feed ships' crews. But the Spanish had also given the Galápagos Islands another name. They called them Las Islas Encantadas, the Enchanted Islands, because sailors said that they seemed to move about as if by magic. As a young scientist, Darwin knew that the "movement" of the Enchanted Islands was an illusion caused by swift, strong ocean currents that flowed among them and made them difficult to approach. During the month he spent in the islands, though, he would discover his own kind of enchantment there.

The first island Darwin explored was Chatham, also known as San Cristóbal. (In Darwin's time, most travelers called the islands by English names. Today their Spanish names are used.) There, Darwin went ashore, noting with discomfort that the ground consisted of sharp lava cinders, so hot that they burned his feet through his boots. As he looked around, he found that the place was not quite as barren as it had appeared from a distance. The offshore waters teemed with sharks and other fish, as the sailors

The huge tortoises of the Galápagos Islands. Darwin discovered that the varying patterns of their shells held a clue to the mystery of how different species are formed.

aboard the Beagle discovered as soon as they lowered their fishing lines. Ashore, not all of the stunted bushes and shrubs were leafless. Some of them, in fact, were in full bloom—but their leaves and flowers were far tinier than any Darwin had seen elsewhere. Cacti stood here and there, a few of them tall enough to offer shade from the blazing sun. The coastline that had looked so empty from the ship turned out to be creeping and hissing with life. Huge black lizards crawled about the rocks, and small scarlet crabs scuttled among the lizards, searching for ticks to eat.

Darwin and his assistant, Syms Covington, wandered inland for a little distance and came upon a broad, well-worn path leading up a hill. Following it, they soon discovered who had made the path: tortoises, who in lumbering to and from a water hole over many years had worn the path bare. The travelers encountered two large tortoises, which hissed at them. The creatures were so large that even together Darwin and Covington could not turn them over. Darwin climbed onto one and took a brief, rather wobbly ride. The tortoise seemed untroubled by Darwin's presence and continued on its way at a rate that its rider calculated to be about four miles (6.4 kilometers) a day—"allowing a little time for it to eat on the road," he reported in his journal. Darwin also described the strange effect of seeing the "huge reptiles, surrounded by black lava, the leafless shrubs, and large cacti." It was, he said, like a vision from some ancient time.

After spending nearly a week at Chatham, the *Beagle* went on to Charles, Albemarle, and James islands, or Santa María, Isabela, and San Salvador as they are now called. Each island offered Darwin new sights and experiences. Charles Island was the only one of the Galápagos with human inhabitants; several hundred convicts, mostly political prisoners, had been exiled there by the government of Ecuador, which claimed the islands. Upon climbing up to the convict settlement, Darwin found that the hilltops, which received some moisture from passing clouds, were less barren than the low-lying shores. Tired of cinders and dry sticks, he rejoiced in the sight of lush green tree ferns and rich mud.

Darwin recognized at once that the islands had been formed by volcanic eruptions. On Albemarle Island, he saw "immense deluges of black naked lava" that had flowed out of the volcanoes like tar overflowing from a boiling pot. The fires that had created the islands were not yet dead—jets of smoke still rose from one crater. Darwin's most thorough survey was made on James Island, where he went ashore with Covington and several shipmates to camp and explore for a week while the *Beagle* filled its water casks at another island. During this time, Darwin made a close study of the big black lizards that populated the islands' shores. Now called marine iguanas, they are the only seagoing lizards in the world. Darwin watched them dive from coastal rocks to feed on seaweed, remain underwater for many minutes at a time, and then emerge to sun themselves on the shore. Their cousins, yellow and brown land iguanas, were as large as the marine iguanas and almost as odd in their behavior. They climbed cactus trees to eat the juiciest leaves, and they lived underground in burrows that they dug with their long claws. One day, seeing one of these iguanas half buried in its burrow, Darwin walked up and tweaked its tail. The iguana was "greatly astonished," Darwin reported. It looked around at him as if to say, "What made you pull my tail?"

All of the animals and birds of the Galápagos were strangely unafraid of humans. Darwin, who had been an

"It is a hideous-looking creature," wrote Darwin of the marine iguana. Nevertheless, the young naturalist closely studied the habits of this unique seagoing lizard.

avid hunter of birds in his youth, had never seen creatures so tame. The Galápagos birds did not fly away in alarm when he approached; he even got close enough to one hawk to brush it off a branch with his rifle. He decided that the creatures of the Galápagos felt little fear of humans because most of the islands had no human inhabitants, only occasional visitors. Therefore the animals and birds had not yet learned to be afraid. But if visitors and settlers made a practice of killing birds and animals, Darwin predicted, future generations of Galápagos wildlife would acquire an instinctive fear of humans. They would become as timid and elusive as the birds and animals of Europe or Asia.

Throughout his stay in the Galápagos, Darwin collected as many samples of animals, fish, birds, insects, plants, and seashells as he could. These were carefully packed up to be taken back to England for further study. As he collected and packed his specimens, he noticed a startling fact: Most of the plants and animals were unique, found only in the Galápagos Islands and nowhere else. Whether he looked at reptiles, birds, or ferns, he found a very high percentage of endemic species, as types of plants and animals that live in only one place are called. Although these endemic plants and animals were similar to those found in South America, there were subtle but important differences that set the Galápagos species apart. The Galápagos island group, Darwin realized, was "a little world within itself."

Darwin became aware of another odd fact, too. Not only did the plant and animal species of the Galápagos Islands differ from those of South America, the closest land mass, but the plants and animals of each island were different from those of every other island. Darwin first learned of this when the vice-governor of the islands told him that each island had a unique variety of tortoise, and that he could tell which island a tortoise came from by looking at the shape and patterns of its shell. Darwin noted this comment, but he did not immediately realize its significance. A few years later, however, he would reexamine his collection of specimens and see that they did indeed differ from island to island. This observation helped him form a bold new idea about how the many species of plants and animals on earth had come to be.

Grim though Darwin's first impression of the Galápagos Islands had been, when the *Beagle* sailed on he was almost sorry to leave. He had become fascinated by the strange forms life had taken on those lonely islands, baked by the equatorial sun and bathed in cold Antarctic currents. But the *Beagle* had business elsewhere. On October 20, Captain FitzRoy gave orders to set sail for Tahiti. Knowing that he had not seen all of the islands' curiosities, Darwin regretfully wrote, "It is the fate of most voyagers, no sooner to discover what is most interesting in any locality, than they are hurried from it."

Darwin never returned to the Galápagos Islands, but in the years that followed he visited them in thought many times, seeking an explanation for the uniqueness of the plants and animals he had seen there. Why did so many of them live only in the Galápagos and nowhere else? And why did the species of plants and animals vary from island to island? Such questions would come to form the basis of Darwin's life's work. His genius lay in the fact that he did not simply observe nature, although he was a keen and meticulous observer. Unlike many naturalists, he was not satisfied to collect facts and describe specimens. He went further; he asked "Why?" Darwin sought to discover the principles *behind* the facts, to understand the processes that had shaped the world. As he examined the specimens he had gathered on his voyage, he began to sense that the Galápagos Islands held a key that would unlock some of nature's secrets.

The Galápagos Islands, he believed, were a sort of laboratory, in which nature had performed its most profound experiments. In those islands, he declared, "both in space and time, we seem to be brought somewhat near to that great fact—that mystery of mysteries—the first appearance of new beings on this earth." After returning to England, Charles Darwin devoted the rest of his long life to exploring the mysterious history of life on earth. In the process, he changed our view of the world, and of humankind's place in it. More than 20 years after the *Beagle* left the Galápagos, Darwin rocked 19th-century society with a revolutionary new theory about how species are formed. The revolution he started is not yet over. Darwin's theory of evolution—of how species change, or evolve, over time—made him the most controversial scientist of the age, perhaps the most controversial of all time. And that brief visit to the Galápagos Islands in 1835 was, he said, "the origin of all my views."

Charles Robert Darwin came from a family with a long-established interest in science. One of his grandfathers, Erasmus Darwin (1731–1802), was a successful and prosperous doctor in Lichfield, a city in central England. Erasmus Darwin had acquired from his own father an interest in fossils and natural history, especially botany, the study of plants. His studies led him to believe that all forms of life on earth were related and that they all sprang from a single source. In short, he proposed the idea that species had evolved—an idea that his grandson Charles Darwin was to explore more fully decades later.

Erasmus Darwin wrote about natural history in a series of books: *The Botanic Garden* (1790), *Zoonomia, or the Laws of Organic Life* (1794–96), and *The Temple of Nature* (1803). He read widely and took an enormous interest in nature—traits that his grandson was to share. Erasmus Darwin also tinkered with mechanical engineering, inventing a new kind of windmill and a carriage that could turn at high speeds without tipping over. He was elected to the prestigious Royal Society, whose membership was limited to England's leading thinkers; he was the first of six generations of his family to

be elected to the society. In addition, Erasmus Darwin helped start his own thinkers' club in the Lichfield area. It was called the Lunar Society because it met on nights when the moon was full, so that the members could travel home at night by moonlight. Darwin and the other members jokingly called themselves "the Lunatics," but they were far from insane—although some of them were visionaries. The club included James Watt, the inventor of the steam engine; Joseph Priestley, England's foremost chemist in the 18th century; and William Small, a physician and astronomer who had spent some time in America, where he was one of Thomas Jefferson's teachers. The members of the Lunar Society shared a passion for new inventions and industries. They believed in knowledge and reason, in freedom of thought, and in progress. They and others like them helped usher in the industrial revolution, sweeping England and the world into a new age of technology.

In the 1760s, while Erasmus Darwin was promoting the construction of a new canal through the fast-growing industrial districts of central England, he got to know Josiah Wedgwood, founder of the well-known Wedgwood firm of pottery manufacturers. The two men became the best of friends, frequently visiting one another's homes. Their friendship was the first bond between the Darwin and Wedgwood families, which have been closely connected ever since.

One of Erasmus Darwin's sons, Robert Waring Darwin, was born in 1766, about the time Erasmus Darwin and Josiah Wedgwood were becoming friends. Thirty years later, Robert Waring Darwin forged another bond between the two families by marrying Susannah Wedgwood, one of Josiah's daughters. Robert and Susannah Darwin settled in a large house called The Mount in the town of Shrewsbury, not far from the Darwin and Wedgwood family homes. There they raised a family of four daughters and two sons.

The Mount, near Shrewsbury, England, was Charles Darwin's childhood home.

The first boy was named Erasmus, in honor of Robert's father. The second, born on February 12, 1809, was called Charles Robert.

Charles's mother died when he was eight years old. His memories of her were few and vague. In 1838 he wrote, "I scarcely recollect anything . . . except being sent for, the memory of going into her room, my father meeting me— crying afterwards. I recollect my mother's gown and scarcely anything of her appearance, except one or two walks with her." After Susannah Darwin's death, her eldest daughters, Caroline, Marianne, and Susan, took over the running of the household. They also took charge of Charles and his younger sister, Catherine. Their attitude toward Charles was kind and loving, but it was also bossy and sometimes a bit oppressive. Charles's older brother, Erasmus, or Ras, escaped most of the girls' mothering because he lived at school.

Life in the Darwin household was dominated by the towering figure of Dr. Robert, as Robert Darwin was called. Like the first Erasmus Darwin, Dr. Robert was a physician with a successful medical practice. He was an imposing man, very tall and immensely fat, with a grave expression and a serious manner. He was adored by his patients, who found him full of kindly sympathy. His wife's death, however, left him sad and irritable, and the Darwin children occasionally found their father rather stiff and severe. "The atmosphere at The Mount was one of never-ending gloom," wrote one of the Wedgwood cousins after a visit. Nevertheless, Charles idolized Dr. Robert and hoped to make his father proud of him. Throughout his life he spoke of his father with great affection and respect. Late in his own life, long after Dr. Robert's death, Charles passed The Mount and was shown through his childhood home by its new owners. As he left, he said wistfully, "If I could have been left alone in that greenhouse for five minutes, I know I should have been able to see my father . . . as vividly as if he had been there before me."

Dr. Robert, as Darwin's father was called, could appear rather forbidding, but Darwin remembered him lovingly as "the kindest man I ever knew."

Unlike Charles's grandfather, Dr. Robert was not especially interested in natural history, although he liked gardening. Dr. Robert passed his fondness for plants on to young Charles, whose lifelong love of flowers started early. A portrait of Charles that was painted when he was seven years old shows him, bright-eyed and rosy-cheeked, dressed in a velvet suit with a lace collar, proudly holding a potted plant. Around this time he was given his own small garden, and he tended it with care.

The natural world, young Charles saw, was full of marvels and fascinating details. He eagerly collected shells, bird's eggs, rocks and minerals, and insects. When he was ten he spent three weeks at the seashore; the most memorable part of this vacation for him was the new insects he spotted. (His first efforts to collect them were thwarted by his sister

Charles and his younger sister, Catherine. The young Darwins were raised by their older sisters after their mother's death.

Susan, who told him it was wrong to kill insects for his collection. For a while he could collect only those he found dead.) Charles also took up fishing and birdwatching. All of these hobbies laid the foundation for his later work, giving him a deep familiarity with nature and teaching him the habit of patient, systematic observation. When he was about 15 he learned to shoot, and for years he loved to hunt partridges and other birds. Although he took up hunting as a gentleman's sport, he later put his skill with the rifle to scientific use in collecting specimens.

Charles's brother, Ras, who planned to be a doctor in the family tradition, also dabbled in science. He turned a toolshed into a chemistry lab and let Charles help with his experiments. In his *Autobiography,* written in 1876, Charles called these efforts "the best part of my education" because they taught him "the meaning of experimental science." They also earned him the nickname "Gas" when his schoolmates learned that he and Ras were experimenting with gases.

Young Charles Darwin did not think much of school. As was true of most children of middle-class families in the early 19th century, his education began at home with his older siblings as his teachers. At the age of eight he began going to a small day school near The Mount. He found his studies there uninteresting but enjoyed boasting to the other boys about his natural history collections. Later he recalled that he sometimes made up ridiculous stories just to get attention. Some of these childhood fibs bore a remarkable relation to the scientific subjects that later held his interest. For example, he invented descriptions of strange birds, and he once claimed that he could change the color of flowers.

In 1818, when Charles was nine years old, he was sent to Shrewsbury School, the private school that Ras attended. Charles spent seven years there, living at school but often running home for casual visits with his family, as the school was less than a mile from The Mount. Later he wrote, "Nothing could have been worse for the development of my mind" than Shrewsbury School. The subjects that interested him—natural history and science—were completely ignored in favor of Greek and Roman history and literature, which were then considered the only subjects essential to a gentlemanly education. The boys spent hours memorizing long passages in dead languages. Charles escaped the boredom by reading Shakespeare's plays or Lord Byron's poems, by daydreaming over travel books, and by taking long, solitary walks to collect rocks and insects. On holidays he and Ras worked at their chemistry experiments or took off on joyous horseback trips with their Wedgwood cousins, riding into the mountains of Wales.

Ras left Shrewsbury School in 1822 to study medicine at Christ's College in Cambridge. Charles carried on alone with chemistry for a while, but he felt listless and bored. He was beginning to think about his future, and he was uncomfortably aware that his father was thinking about it, too. Charles had not distinguished himself at Shrewsbury School. Dr. Robert feared that he would grow up into an idle sportsman. "You care for nothing but shooting, dogs, and rat-catching, and you will be a disgrace to yourself and all your family," the doctor reproached Charles. But Dr. Robert thought he knew what Charles needed. He took Charles out of Shrewsbury School two years ahead of schedule and announced that the 16-year-old boy was going to be a doctor. His medical studies would start at once.

Edinburgh, Scotland, hailed as "the northern Athens" during the early 19th century, offered new intellectual freedoms and challenges to 16-year-old Charles Darwin.

CHAPTER

2

The Restless Searcher

Robert Darwin decided to send Charles to medical school at Edinburgh University in Scotland. Dr. Robert had studied there, and so had Erasmus Darwin, Charles's grandfather. To Charles's great delight, his brother, Ras, was also sent to Edinburgh to complete his own medical studies. The two young men arrived in Edinburgh in October 1825, found rooms in a lodging house near the university, warily tasted such Scottish delicacies as fish heads stuffed with oatmeal, and threw themselves into the city's intellectual life.

Edinburgh was called "the northern Athens" because, like the Athens of ancient Greece, it was a cosmopolitan center of learning. Free thought and new ideas were tolerated there more than in England because Scottish intellectual life was not dominated by religion. Students and teachers at the English universities in Cambridge and Oxford were required to announce their belief in the state religion, the Church of England, which was not only one of the pillars of the English monarchy but also a powerful unifying force in society. In England, the church discouraged speculation about the age of the earth or the history of living things, claiming that such matters were properly explained by the Bible, not by science. But students and teachers in Scotland were not bound by an official religion. Furthermore, Scotland had long had close cultural and political ties with France, home of some of the most innovative philosophers and scientists of the 18th century, and Edinburgh's intellectual life was enriched by the presence of teachers from Paris and elsewhere in Europe.

Edinburgh, with its free-thinking atmosphere, was a hotbed of activity in geology, the study of the earth, and biology, the study of life. Physicians, writers, philosophers, and naturalists from all over Great Britain, Europe, and even the United States gathered in Edinburgh. To the end of his life Charles Darwin remembered seeing the American naturalist John James Audubon, dressed in the rough clothes of a backwoodsman, with his black hair streaming over his collar, demonstrating the proper way to mount a stuffed bird. All in all, Edinburgh was a heady, stimulating place for a young man beginning to explore the world of ideas and science.

The two Darwins attacked their studies with zeal. During their first term, they took more books out of the university library than any other students; they also bought books with their generous allowance from Dr. Robert. Their enthusiasm, however, did not last long. Charles complained that the lectures were painfully dull, but far greater horrors awaited him in the operating rooms. In the days before painkilling anesthetics, surgery was performed on patients who were strapped to their beds, often conscious and terrified, with buckets of sawdust on hand to absorb the blood. The medical students were expected to watch operations, but Charles was unable to stand the sight of the blood and the screams of the patients. He tried twice, but after viewing an especially gruesome operation on a child he fled the room, never to return. Although later in life he was sorry that he had never properly learned the art of dissection, which would have been useful to him in his scientific studies, he never overcame his dread of blood and pain.

Charles was happy when the school year ended. He spent the summer visiting his Wedgwood cousins and other friends, and enjoying all his favorite hobbies. He was so fond of hunting and shooting that, as he later recalled, he kept his hunting boots ready by his bed "so as not to lose half a minute in putting them on in the morning." In later years, though, he lost his pleasure in shooting. "I discovered," he explained, "that the pleasure of observing & reasoning was a much higher one than that of skill & sport."

Ras did not return to Edinburgh after that first year; instead, he went to London to finish his medical degree. Charles believed that Ras would never practice medicine, and events proved him right. Dr. Robert decided that Ras's health was too delicate to allow him to work, so Ras settled into a life of comfortable leisure in London, where he pursued friendships with leading literary and scientific figures.

Charles prepared to go back to Edinburgh for his second year of medical school, although he had began to suspect that he, too, might never become a doctor. He knew that he would inherit a substantial sum from his father, who had grown rich by investing in land. The knowledge that he would have plenty of money to live on and would not need to worry about supporting himself as a physician made medical school less appealing than ever. During his second year at Edinburgh, he devoted more energy to natural history than to medicine.

In 1826, Charles joined the Plinian Society, a club for men interested in natural history. At the society's meetings, long-established notions were hotly challenged by daring new ideas. In religious terms, the debate was between orthodox, or traditional, thinking and heretical, or radical, thinking. Orthodox thinkers—by far the majority in science and in society at large—accepted the Bible as the literal truth. They believed that the world had been shaped by God through miracles and supernatural forces, such as

Noah's great flood. Many people of Darwin's time believed that this and other events had occurred exactly as described in the Bible. Scientific thinkers, however, were beginning to challenge the biblical view of the earth's history.

divine creation and Noah's great flood. The heretics, on the other hand, rejected supernatural and divine explanations for things. Science, they insisted, could explain the world in terms of understandable physical forces—natural forces such as chemical reactions and gravity. The radical thinkers also claimed that man was part of the natural world, not a special creation standing apart from it.

Conservative, orthodox thinkers were frightened and angered by those who questioned the traditional view of the world. They called the new ideas mechanistic because they felt that the radical view of life reduced man to a mere mechanism without a soul. The traditionalists also feared that the new ideas might tear apart the fabric of society, which was held together by the church. Look what had happened in France, they warned: Free thought and radical ideas had run wild during the 18th century, encouraging the lower classes to question the established order of things—and the century had ended with the bloody French Revolution.

Plinian Society meetings were frequently enlivened by arguments between traditional and radical thinkers—arguments that ranged over politics, philosophy, and religion as well as scientific questions. At the first meeting Darwin attended, for example, a member named William Browne criticized a new book that claimed that God had given humans special muscles so that people could smile, frown, and laugh. Browne declared that this was nonsense. Humans and animals, he argued, had the same kinds of muscles—a most heretical, radical notion.

Darwin's contribution to science must be viewed against the background of the great struggle of ideas that was raging in the scientific world as he came of age. Darwin was deeply troubled by the conflict between old and new ideas; he held back from making his ideas public, even when he was convinced that they were sound, because he knew that they would cause an uproar and he hated to be the center of controversy. In another way, though, this struggle of ideas helped Darwin by providing a fertile environment in which his mind could be stimulated. Like all great thinkers, Darwin was influenced by the work of other people. His brilliant insights into the nature of living things were shaped, in part, by the books and scientific papers that were published in his day and by the discussions and debates they sparked. Darwin was not a lone visionary on a mountaintop, grasping truths that no one else had seen; he was a product of his time, and his ideas grew out of the intellectual climate in which he lived. Today, Darwin is remembered as the founder of the theory of evolution, but ideas about evolution had been discussed for years before Darwin came along. It happened, however, that Darwin brought his rare intellect to science at a particularly fruitful time.

For centuries, Western thought had been based on the Bible, which says that God created the earth and everything on it in six days. This creation, moreover, was supposed to have happened just a few thousand years earlier. In the 17th century many scholars, including the English mathematician Isaac Newton, added up all the generations named in the Bible and decided that the earth had been created four or five thousand years before the birth of Christ. Archbishop James Ussher of Armagh, Ireland, concluded that creation had occurred in 4004 B.C., a date that became famous because it was printed in so many Bibles that most people, including Charles Darwin, thought it was part of the original biblical text.

By Darwin's time, many observant and thoughtful people had questioned the biblical account of creation. The first challenge came from geology. Fossils—rocks that bore an uncanny resemblance to shells and other living things—had long been a source of mystery. What were they, and where did they come from? It was once thought that fossils were simply rocks that happened by coincidence to be shaped like plants and animals. By the 18th century, however, geologists had realized that fossils were the actual relics of once-living things. But how could they have turned to stone in just a few thousand years?

The mystery deepened when people began unearthing fossils that clearly bore no relation to any living creatures. The most spectacular were the fossils of dinosaurs, the first of which was discovered by an English couple named Gideon and Mary Ann Mantell in 1822. Soon more dinosaur fossils were found, and they captured the public imagination with their great size and strangeness. It became obvious that the earth had once been home to forms of life that no longer existed. But how could this be, if, as orthodox thinkers claimed, God had created each species in its final form once and for all time? Orthodox Christians met this challenge by claiming that the extinct creatures had drowned in the great flood described in the Bible. For example, Robert FitzRoy, captain of the *Beagle,* believed that mammoths had become extinct because they were too large to fit into the doorway of Noah's ark. This is why 19th-century writers often described dinosaurs, mammoths, and other extinct animals as "antediluvian" (which means "before the deluge," or flood).

A theory called catastrophism held that the earth's history had consisted of a series of catastrophes, or sudden, devastating events, such as worldwide floods, volcanic eruptions, and earthquakes. According to the catastrophists, every aspect of the earth's appearance, from mountains to canyons, resulted from a past catastrophe. Catastrophism explained why fossils of seashells were sometimes found on mountaintops far from the sea: They had been washed there by floods. The religious version of catastrophism held that God had created and destroyed the world many times, and that the creation described in the Bible was only the most recent one. The dinosaurs and other extinct animals belonged to earlier creations and had perished in the destruction that preceded each new creation.

A rival theory about the earth's history emerged in the late 18th century. In 1788, a Scottish intellectual named James Hutton (1726–97) published a long scientific paper called "Theory of the Earth"; it was reissued as a book in 1795. Hutton claimed that the present state of the earth could best be explained not by immense, dramatic convulsions in the past, but by the slow, steady action of familiar forces over a very long period of time. According to Hutton, the earth was shaped by these gradual processes. Rivers deposited silt to form new layers of soil; seas slowly dried up, and over thousands of years their beds were pushed up into mountain ranges, complete with fossil shells. Because Hutton said that geological processes took place at a steady, uniform rate rather than in a series of catastrophic lurches, his theory was called uniformitarianism.

Uniformitarianism made the earth much older than anyone had previously believed. Hutton's earth-shaping

text continues on page 34

The death of a plant or animal sometimes means more than the passing of an individual organism. Occasionally it is also the death of an entire species. When the last dusky seaside sparrow died in Florida on June 16, 1987, that particular kind of North American songbird was extinct—gone forever.

The idea that a species could pass out of existence was hard for many people to accept because it seemed to contradict theology. But by the late 18th century, naturalists were beginning to agree that extinction had occurred many times in the earth's history. Fossils of extinct creatures—especially dinosaurs and other huge beasts that had once roamed the earth—filled people with wonder. Darwin, who unearthed fossils of several "extinct monsters" in South America, wrote in *On the Origin of Species,* "No one I think can have marvelled more at the extinction of species, than I have done."

Scientists now know that extinction has always been part of life. Paleontologist David M. Raup of the University of Chicago estimates that 99.9 percent of all species that have ever existed are now extinct. In the 1980s Raup and his colleague Jack Sepkopski published the results of a detailed study of the fossil record in which they arrived at a "background" rate of extinction—the normal rate at which categories of organisms have become extinct throughout the history of life on earth. But the fossil record also includes at least five "great dyings" or mass extinctions, during which the rate of extinction rose dramatically for periods that were brief in terms of geological time. The biggest mass extinction occurred some 245 to 225 million years ago, when, according to Raup, as many as 96 percent of all existing species died out. Three-fourths of all species, including the last dinosaurs, disappeared in a mass extinction about 65 million years ago.

Scientists have advanced many theories about the great dyings. Some believe that they were caused by changes in the global climate that occurred when the continental plates drifted from tropical to polar regions and back again. Others claim that large asteroids or comets crashed into the earth, creating worldwide dust clouds; these clouds blocked sunlight and lowered the temperature, causing the mass extinctions. Geologists and paleontologists are still examining the evidence for these and other theories.

Extinction is closely related to evolution. As Darwin recognized, fossils of extinct creatures cast light on the connections between species and on the stages by which one form of life gives way to another. Darwin also realized that the birth of new species was linked to the death of existing ones. In the *Origin* he noted that "the appearance of new forms and the disappearance of old forms . . . are closely bound together." Evolutionary biologists continue to offer new ideas about extinction and its role in speciation, or the formation of new species. One influential idea came from Stephen Jay Gould of Harvard University and Niles Eldredge of the American Museum of Natural History. Their theory of punctuated equilibrium ("punk eke" to paleontologists) says that the number of species stays pretty much the same for long periods of time, but occasionally this state of balance, or equilibrium, is broken up, or punctuated, by bursts of rapid speciation. During these bursts, many new species arise suddenly—that is, within a few million years or so. The bursts often occur just after a number of species have become extinct, because extinction makes room for new species to evolve.

Earth is in the midst of another great dying—one that cannot be blamed on an asteroid. The current mass extinction is the work of one astoundingly successful species, *Homo sapiens,* which drives dozens of species into extinction each day through habitat destruction, environmental pollution, and other effects of modern industry and reckless population growth. Perhaps this mass dying will allow new species to flower over the next several million years. But, as Darwin wrote, "a species when once lost should never reappear." The plants, insects, and animals that become extinct today are gone for all time.

text continued from page 31

processes would have needed thousands upon thousands of years to do their job. Summing up his view of geological history, Hutton wrote, "The result, therefore, of our present enquiry is, that we find no vestige of a beginning—no prospect of an end."

This view of the earth's history as stretching far back into an unimaginably ancient past confused and disturbed people who were accustomed to thinking of history in brief, biblical terms. As Hutton's friend John Playfair wrote in 1802, "The mind seemed to grow giddy by looking so far into the abyss of time." Yet by the 1820s uniformitarianism was gaining ground because it explained features of geology that catastrophism could not explain.

Today geologists know that *both* uniformitarianism and catastrophism are true. Geological changes take place slowly and over long periods of time, as when rainfall erodes a mountain range a little at a time or a glacier grinds forward at a snail's pace, but sudden cataclysms such as floods and volcanic eruptions also have helped to shape the earth. In Darwin's day, however, the vision of uniformitarianism— the unfolding of the millions of past years that geologists call "deep time"—was considered revolutionary. A few years after Darwin left Edinburgh, he would be profoundly influenced by an important new book that supported Hutton's vision of deep time.

While geologists were delving into the distant past, biologists were challenging the orthodox notions about life. Traditionally, the forms of living things had been viewed as fixed and unchanging. Both religion and natural history arranged the various species neatly in a ladder of life. At the bottom of the ladder were "low" creatures such as earthworms and insects. Reptiles, birds, and mammals occupied ever-higher rungs. Humans were perched at the very pinnacle of the ladder, right below the angels.

To those who believed in the biblical view of life, the orderliness and structural perfection of nature seemed to prove that God had created the natural world. This idea is called the "argument from design," or the "watchmaker argument." In his 1802 book *Natural Theology,* Bishop William Paley outlined the argument: Suppose you were out walking and came upon a pocket watch. You had never seen a watch before. Seeing that the watch was a precise, intricate mechanism, you would conclude that it could not simply have happened at random. It must have been designed and made by a watchmaker. The eye, like the pocket watch, is a delicate, intricate mechanism. It is so perfect that it, too, must have been designed, and its designer was God. In his youth Darwin was "charmed and convinced" by Paley's argument. Later in his career, however, he pointed out its weaknesses.

New discoveries and ideas kept casting fresh doubt on the notion that each species had been created by God in a perfect, permanent form. What about the extinct species? If they were perfect, why did they disappear? And what about the new kinds of plants and animals that explorers were finding in Africa, Australia, and the Americas? These were not mentioned in the Bible. Had God performed a separate act of creation for each continent? A few scholars, seeing how easily farmers and stock breeders created new varieties of fruit, flowers, and poultry, realized that species were fluid and changeable, not fixed and unchanging. Darwin's own grandfather, Erasmus Darwin, had this insight. So did Jean-Baptiste Lamarck (1744–1829), a French zoologist-philosopher who wrote that species adapt, or change, to fit their environment. But Lamarck could not convincingly describe *how* these changes took place.

Charles Darwin was exposed to the theories of Lamarck and of his grandfather while he was in Edinburgh, but he does not seem to have been very much impressed by them. (Throughout his career Darwin insisted, not altogether convincingly, that his own work had not been influenced by Erasmus Darwin's writings. Scholars are still studying the relationship between the two men's ideas.) The teenage Darwin was far from being an evolutionist. In his autobiography, he claimed that in the 1820s he still believed in "the strict and literal truth of every word in the Bible." At that time, Darwin had not begun to think about the big picture of life on earth. He was still entranced by its tiny, fascinating details.

He spent hours studying the stuffed birds in the university's natural history museum or hiking over cliffs and hills, poking at rocks and trying to piece together the local geology. With friends from the Plinian Society, he made expeditions along the seashore; they waited until the tide was far out to scour the sands for sponges, sea pens, and other small creatures washed up from the deep. Sometimes when the fishermen took their trawlers out to dredge for oysters, Darwin accompanied them and squatted on the slippery decks while he sifted through their haul for sea slugs. In March 1827 he proudly reported to the Plinian Society several discoveries he had made concerning the structure of microscopic sea organisms.

Darwin spent the summer of 1827 traveling and relaxing. He made his first visit to London, which he called a "horrid smoky wilderness." Together with his uncle Josiah Wedgwood II and his cousins Emma and Fanny, he made his first and only trip to the European continent, spending several weeks in Paris. But the question of his future weighed heavily upon him. He was restless and tired of medical school, where he had not done well in his classes. Dr. Robert realized that Charles had no desire to become a doctor, but he felt that the boy should have *some* position in society. Although Dr. Robert was not a religious man, he knew that the Church of England (also called the Anglican Church) provided a secure and respectable way of life for its clergymen. He decided that Charles should enter the church.

"Considering how fiercely I have been attacked by the

orthodox," Darwin wrote late in life, "it seems ludicrous that I once intended to be a clergyman." Darwin would find himself at odds with the church in the 1850s, but in 1827 he was happy to agree to his father's new plan. Although he did not have strong religious feelings, he was aware that the life of a country clergyman offered considerable leisure in which he could pursue his interest in natural history. In fact, many of the leading naturalists of the day were clergymen, for science was not yet established as a profession in its own right, and it was almost impossible to earn a living through scientific work alone.

But before Darwin could become a clergyman-naturalist, he needed more education. He enrolled in Christ's College at Cambridge and found to his dismay that he had to hire a tutor to refresh his knowledge of the Greek and Latin he had paid so little attention to at Shrewsbury School. His exams were grueling, and each one threw Darwin into a panic, although by studying furiously he managed to pass them all.

Cambridge offered a lively social life to a young man with pocket money and a friendly disposition. Darwin drifted into what he called "a sporting set," a group of young men who enjoyed riding and shooting. Later he looked back fondly on their lively dinner parties, which featured "jolly singing and playing at cards afterwards." He wrote sheepishly, "I know that I ought to feel ashamed of days and evenings thus spent, but as some of my friends were very pleasant, and we were all in the highest spirits, I cannot help looking back to those times with much pleasure."

Studying and revelry did not take up all of Darwin's time. His interest in natural history had a new focus: beetles. He and his cousin William

Albert Way, a beetle-hunting friend of Darwin and his cousin William Darwin Fox, drew this sketch of Darwin "beetling."

Darwin Fox, also a student at Christ's College, became obsessed with beetle hunting, which they called "beetling." Darwin went to great lengths to secure new specimens. He paid a local laborer to gather water beetles from the bottoms of riverboats—and fired him indignantly when he learned that the man had turned the best specimens over to a rival collector in exchange for a bribe.

On one beetling expedition, Darwin saw two rare beetles and seized one in each hand. Then he saw a third species. Unwilling to let any of them escape, he popped the beetle in his right hand into his mouth so that he could grab the new specimen. The beetle in his mouth reacted by squirting out a vile, bitter fluid. Appalled, Darwin spat out his victim, and in the confusion he lost the third beetle as well. On another outing he captured a beetle that brought him better luck. It turned out to be a new species, and a scientific journal gave Darwin credit for capturing the first known specimen. Decades later, the world-renowned Darwin called that modest early triumph "the proudest moment of my life."

At Cambridge, Darwin got to know two influential clergymen-scientists, the botanist John Stevens Henslow and the geologist Adam Sedgwick. Darwin learned much about plants and insects from Henslow; the two spent so much time walking in the Cambridge countryside that Darwin was identified as "the man who walks with Henslow." Later Darwin was to say that his friendship with Henslow was the most important influence on his entire career. Sedgwick, too, broadened Darwin's intellectual horizons by teaching him about field geology. Darwin was impressed by the older man's ability to read the earth's history from the rocks. Listening to Sedgwick, he suddenly saw science in a new way. A scientist, Darwin realized, must do more than just record facts; he must also search for patterns of meaning. "Nothing before had ever made me thoroughly realise, though I had read various scientific books, that science con-

sists in grouping facts so that general laws or conclusions may be drawn from them," Darwin wrote
of one field trip with Sedgwick.

Darwin's final examinations were scheduled
for January 1831. Study and anxiety made him
miserable for weeks beforehand, but when the
results were posted, he ranked 10th in a class of
178. Jubilantly, with his degree in hand, he set off
on a geological expedition to Wales with
Sedgwick, then returned to The Mount to spend
the summer with his father and sisters.

At the age of 22, Charles Darwin was a healthy, vigor-
ous young man, just under six feet tall. His brown eyes were
deeply set under a high, bulging forehead; his light brown
hair was thin and short, but his side-whiskers were fashion-
ably long and bushy. A mild, easygoing fellow, he seemed
headed straight for the placid life of a country clergyman.
Then, on August 29, 1831, he received a letter that changed
the course of his life.

Botanist John Stevens Henslow. The countryside rambles that Darwin and Henslow shared at Cambridge helped lay the foundation for Darwin's scientific career.

3

The Voyage of the *Beagle*

The letter that Darwin received on that fateful day was from John Stevens Henslow. It contained a remarkable offer: a chance for Darwin to sail around the world. The British navy ship *Beagle* was being sent to South America to make coastal surveys. From there the ship would return to England by way of the Pacific and Indian oceans. The *Beagle's* captain, 26-year-old Robert FitzRoy, wanted someone to keep him company during the three-year voyage, which would offer outstanding opportunities for natural history study in many parts of the globe. Henslow had recommended Darwin. Was Darwin interested?

Indeed he was. At Cambridge Darwin had read the works of Alexander von Humboldt (1769–1859), a German naturalist who was hailed as one of the world's foremost scientific travelers. Darwin's imagination was fired by Humboldt's descriptions of South American rain forests and volcanoes; he longed to see some of these faraway wonders for himself. He was wildly excited when he read Henslow's letter. But his diary for the next day contains only the words "Refused offer of Voyage." Behind that curt sentence lay a world of frustration.

The Beagle near Tierra del Fuego, at the southern tip of South America. "I never saw a more cheerless prospect,"
wrote Darwin of this harsh, desolate landscape.

Dr. Robert had turned down his son's hopeful request for permission to make the trip. There were many objections to the scheme, as Charles had admitted. The voyage would be costly, for Darwin would have to pay for his own scientific equipment and meals. It would also be uncomfortable and dangerous. Many travelers perished from tropical diseases or from disasters at sea; indeed, the *Beagle* was a small brig, a class of ships so accident-prone that they were nicknamed "floating coffins." Other men had been offered the trip, and they had turned it down—perhaps with excellent reason. Finally, the doctor feared that years of travel and adventure would make his son unwilling to settle down to the quiet life of a clergyman. Darwin, who respected his father's judgment and was always eager to win his approval, swallowed his disappointment and wrote to Henslow that he could not accept the offer. He added, "But if it had not been for my Father, I would have taken all risks."

One loophole remained open. Dr. Robert had said, "If you can find any man of common-sense who advises you to

In a letter dated August 31, 1831, Darwin told his father that his uncle, Josiah Wedgwood II, was in favor of the Beagle voyage. Dr. Robert thereupon gave Darwin permission to make the trip—thus changing the course of scientific history.

go I will give my consent." To Darwin's great joy, his uncle Josiah Wedgwood II—whom Dr. Robert had always considered very sensible—thought the voyage would be a good thing. It would let Darwin see something of the world and expand his scientific work at the same time. When Dr. Robert learned of Wedgwood's favorable opinion, he immediately gave Darwin his gracious consent. Darwin was profoundly grateful. He was also mindful of the fact that he had spent a great deal of his father's money at Cambridge and would now spend still more of it. He joked that he would have to be "deuced clever" to spend much money aboard ship. "But they tell me," his father replied with a smile, "that you are very clever."

Darwin plunged into a whirlwind of activity. There was much to do, for the *Beagle* was scheduled to set sail in October. Darwin rushed to London to meet FitzRoy. A few days later FitzRoy showed Darwin around the ship that would be his home for the next few years. Darwin was rather taken aback to discover that the *Beagle*, which would carry 74 men, was only 90 feet long; his quarters would consist of one corner of a small cabin, and he would have to sleep in a hammock. Still, the *Beagle* was clean and well

A sketch of the Beagle, *showing FitzRoy and Darwin at the table in the captain's cabin.*

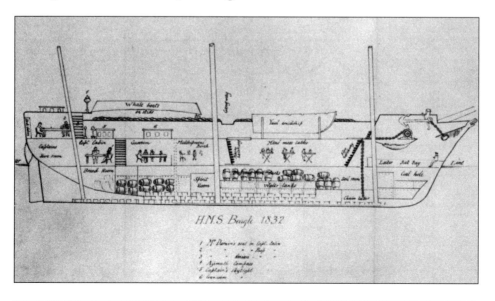

H.M.S. Beagle 1832

equipped. The prospect of a long voyage in the little vessel distressed Darwin, but in a letter to his sisters he enthusiastically described FitzRoy as the "ideal" captain. The two men seemed to hit it off well—which was fortunate, because it was FitzRoy who determined whether Darwin would make the voyage.

Darwin is sometimes called the *Beagle's* naturalist, but this is not quite accurate. He had no official standing at all; in fact, his presence on the *Beagle* is an example of how science in the early 19th century was largely an amateur pastime for wealthy gentlemen. Although by this time the missions of most naval expeditions included some natural history, the navy rarely employed naturalists to gather biological and geological specimens during voyages. Instead, ship's officers were encouraged to develop an interest in natural history so that they could carry out some scientific work as well as their regular duties. This responsibility generally fell on ships' doctors, and Dr. Robert McCormick, the surgeon aboard the *Beagle*, was the ship's official naturalist. But the navy also allowed civilian naturalists to accompany many voyages at their own expense.

In the case of the *Beagle*, FitzRoy wanted to find a private passenger for the voyage because the rules of naval etiquette prevented the captain from having any social contact with the officers and crew; furthermore, as a descendant of King Charles II, FitzRoy was very proud of his status and felt that no one in the ship's company belonged to his social class. He needed a gentleman of the proper background and breeding to serve as his companion primarily so that he would not have to eat dinner alone for three years or longer. Darwin was expected to take his meals in the captain's cabin, to be available for conversation when FitzRoy felt sociable, and to assemble a natural history collection that would contribute to the overall glory of the voyage. He felt quite capable of performing all of these duties. As it happened, McCormick left the *Beagle* after only a few months,

annoyed because Darwin had more leisure and resources than he did to devote to collecting and studying specimens. Thereafter Darwin was the *Beagle*'s sole naturalist, although he received much good-natured help from the officers and crew.

Before leaving England, Darwin hastily assembled his gear. His shirts and socks required little storage space, but the same could not be said of his scientific equipment: dissecting tools, chemicals, and special boxes and jars for preserving plant and animal specimens; carefully packed instruments, including microscopes, a telescope, a compass, and a barometer; a hammer for chipping geological samples and a net for trawling specimens from the sea; and rifles for shooting birds and animals, as well as a pair of pistols, purchased on FitzRoy's advice as protection against South American bandits and South Pacific cannibals, which made Darwin feel quite dashing. Darwin also brought aboard a library of scientific books. One of these, a farewell gift from Henslow, was the first volume of an important new work called *Principles of Geology* by Charles Lyell, who is regarded as the founder of modern geology. Lyell's work supported the uniformitarian idea that the earth's history stretched far back into deep time. During the voyage, Darwin devoured *Principles of Geology,* and Lyell's insights helped him understand the new geological formations he encountered.

With much ingenuity, Darwin managed to get all of his belongings stowed aboard the *Beagle.* He made his farewells to family and friends and promised to write regularly to his sisters—a promise that he was to keep diligently. The *Beagle* made several attempts to depart but was twice turned back to port by bad weather. Darwin grew almost unbearably restless in his cramped quarters. The weather depressed him, he was lonely and homesick, and shipboard life was more difficult than he had expected. He had a hard time mastering his hammock, which had a tendency to sling him out onto the chart table, and an even harder time mastering his upset stomach, for Darwin had discovered, to his distress, that he was extremely prone to seasickness.

When the *Beagle* finally got underway on December 27, Darwin was so ill that for days he could do nothing but lie limply in his hammock, nibbling cautiously at raisins and biscuits between bouts of nausea. He had never been so miserable. The great adventure was off to a decidedly unglamorous start.

Matters soon improved. Darwin never completely overcame his seasickness, but within a couple of weeks he was feeling better and was able to take an interest in his surroundings. He found that shipboard life, with its snugness and its familiar daily routine, had considerable charm. "I find a ship a very comfortable house, with everything you want," he wrote to his father, "and if it were not for sea-sickness the whole world would be sailors."

As planned, the *Beagle* sailed around the world, but not straight around. The ship spent three years surveying the little-known coastlines of Argentina and Chile, working in the southern latitudes near Tierra del Fuego during the summers and retreating northward to warmer waters during the winters. Darwin visited many places—including the Falkland Islands and Tierra del Fuego—more than once. Because the *Beagle* made multiple visits to many ports, Darwin was often able to spend several weeks or months ashore while the ship worked its way back and forth along the coast. During some of these shore visits, Darwin made ambitious overland journeys. While the *Beagle* was on the east coast of South America, he rode on horseback for 600 miles (960 kilometers) across the pampas, the vast grassy plains of Argentina. Later, when the ship was surveying the west coast of the continent, he led his own small expedition across the towering Andes Mountains and back.

text continues on page 51

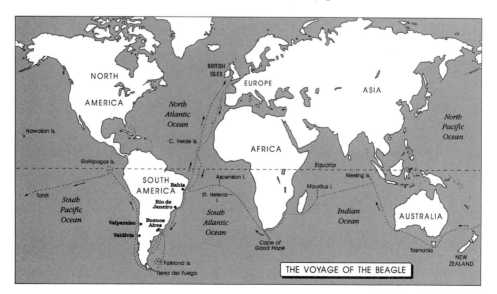

THE VOYAGE OF THE BEAGLE

Any discussion of Darwin's work contains numerous references to *species*. The word even appears in the title of the book that introduced his theory of evolution: *On the Origin of Species* (1859). Yet in the *Origin,* Darwin admitted that nobody really knew exactly what a species was. "No one definition has as yet satisfied all naturalists," he wrote, "yet every naturalist knows vaguely what he means when he speaks of a species."

The species is the basic unit of biological taxonomy, which is the science of placing plants and animals into categories based on their similarities and differences. The foundation of modern taxonomy was laid by a Swedish scholar named Carolus Linnaeus (1707–78), who spent his life classifying living things. He divided all life into two large groups—the plant kingdom and the animal kingdom. (Modern biologists recognize five kingdoms: plants, animals, fungi, and two kingdoms of tiny single-celled organisms.) These broad categories are subdivided into a series of progressively smaller categories: phyla, classes, orders, families, genera, and species. Biologists sometimes add extra levels such as subphyla, subfamilies, and subspecies (or varieties).

Linnaeus also invented the system of two-part Latin names that is still used today to identify species. The first part of the name identifies the genus, or group of related species, to which the organism belongs. The second word identifies the particular species. The genus *Panthera,* for example, includes several kinds of large cats, but the name *Panthera leo* identifies the lion. A third name may be added to identify a subspecies—for example, the Asiatic lion is called *Panthera leo persica.*

Still the question remains: What *is* a species? It is clear from the *Origin* that Darwin, like modern biologists, defined a species as a population of individuals that can mate with one another and produce fertile offspring. Various barriers keep the species from breeding with other species—or, as biologists say, keep it reproductively isolated. The biggest barrier to cross-breeding between species is simply the fact that most species never attempt it. In the majority of cases where cross-species interbreeding *does* occur—as

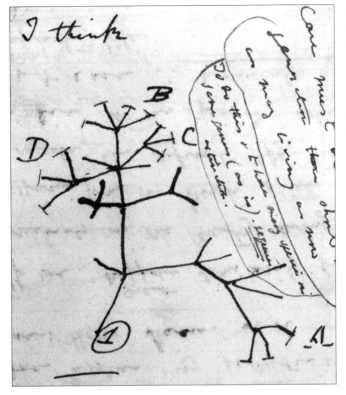

This diagram of an "evolutionary tree" appears in one of Darwin's notebooks from the period 1836–1844, when he was grappling with the questions of how new species are formed by splitting off from a parent stock.

when horses and donkeys mate—the parents are genetically different, and their offspring are sterile. Some species of plants or animals in the wild *can* produce fertile offspring with other closely related species, but their reproductive isolation is enforced by other barriers. They may live in different localities, separated by mountain ranges or rivers; this is called geographic isolation. For example, the various types of tortoise that Darwin encountered on the Galápagos Islands could have bred with one another, but each type was confined to its own island. Species and subspecies that live in the same region may be reproductively isolated by other factors—they may live in different habitats or breed at different seasons.

continued from previous page

Scientists now know that organisms of the same species can inter-breed because they share a common genetic material. Genetic studies are increasingly being used to clarify the relationships among different species; in the 1980s, for example, several teams studying genetic material from apes and humans found that humans and chimpanzees are more closely related to one another than either is to gorillas.

Experiments with breeding and genetic material are not always practical, and biologists have long used other features—such as behavior, color, anatomical structure, and ecological niche—to tell species apart. The borderlines of species are not always clear. Some biologists are called lumpers, for they avoid unnecessary subdivisions and may lump subspecies into the main species; others are known as splitters, because they are prone to make fine distinctions that split groups into smaller groups.

Most of the time, however, the identification of species is remarkably consistent, whether the observer is a highly trained scientist or a local hunter drawing upon traditional lore. On the rain forest island of New Guinea, Western zoologists have sighted more than 700 bird species. Some of these species are extremely hard to identify without close physical examination. Yet time after time, the scientists have been astonished to learn that the islanders, using subtle clues in the birds' behavior and habitat, can easily tell them apart.

text continued from page 47

For Darwin, the voyage was truly a journey of discovery. Everything interested him; everything he saw enlarged his vision of the natural world. The *Beagle* reached Brazil in February 1832 and spent four months there before heading south. Darwin was intoxicated by his expeditions into Brazil's tropical rain forest, an environment that contains more species of plants and animals than any other on earth. "Delight is a weak term to express the feelings of a naturalist who for the first time has wandered by himself in a Brazilian forest," he wrote in his journal. Gazing around him in rapture, he felt like a blind man who had just been given sight.

The profusion of life in the rain forest was dazzling: one day Darwin captured 68 beetle species, and on another occasion he shot 80 different species of birds in the course of a morning walk. He witnessed the terrifying march of a horde of ravening army ants that devoured everything in its path; he experimented to see whether tree frogs could walk up panes of glass; he measured the trunks of colossal trees. His attention darted from parrots to palms to beetles to orchids. "I am at present red-hot with Spiders," he wrote to Henslow, describing a new enthusiasm. In a letter to his sister Caroline, he spoke gleefully of "the fine miserlike pleasure" he felt when examining an unknown species. The specimens Darwin collected—many of them new to science—were regularly crated up and shipped back to Henslow.

Not all of Darwin's discoveries were pleasant ones. He suffered his first attack of a tropical fever in Brazil, and he also witnessed firsthand the horrors of slavery. Portuguese colonists had imported a large number of African slaves into Brazil; at the time of Darwin's visit, nearly all of the plantation workers and house servants were slaves. The Darwins and the Wedgwoods loathed slavery, and Darwin had absorbed his relatives' views on the subject. He was deeply disturbed when he saw a small slave boy beaten with a horsewhip, or heard a slave owner threaten to sell the wives and children of all his slaves. "I thank God," he wrote after leaving Brazil, "that I shall never again visit a slave country."

The issue of slavery provoked a serious quarrel between Darwin and FitzRoy. The captain argued that slavery was as old as the Bible and that slaves were needed to work large plantations. He claimed that he had visited a plantation where the slaves were happy. The plantation owner had called all the slaves together before FitzRoy and asked them if they would rather be free. All of them, said FitzRoy, had answered "no." Darwin asked scornfully whether FitzRoy thought they would have dared to say anything else in front of their master. FitzRoy lost his temper and ordered Darwin out of his cabin. A few hours later, FitzRoy apologized, but the incident gave Darwin a taste of the captain's temper. Although FitzRoy was an excellent commander, his ship-mates learned to walk warily around him, for he was given to outbursts of anger and fits of moodiness. Later in the voyage, FitzRoy suffered such a severe spell of depression that he almost gave up his command.

The next stage of the *Beagle*'s mission took the ship to Argentina. The windswept plains and the barren, muddy coast were less colorful than the Brazilian forest, but they held much to interest Darwin. At a place called Punta Alta, he saw some old bones embedded in a mound of gravel and clay and started digging with a pickax. He unearthed remarkable fossils of creatures long extinct and unknown to science: giant sloths and armadillos, a hippopotamus-like creature called *Toxodon,* an extinct South American elephant, and more. Darwin called the plains of Argentina "one wide sepulchre of these extinct quadrupeds." He realized that his finds would help scientists piece together a picture of what the world was like ages ago, when the Americas "swarmed with great monsters." Believing that the tapirs, sloths, guanacos, and armadillos of modern South

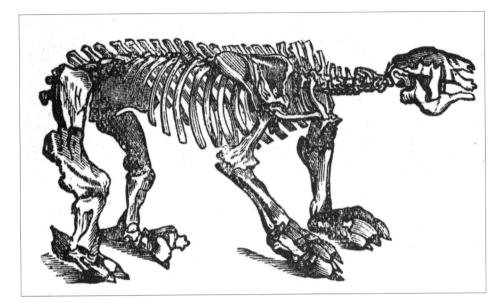

America were descended from the giant creatures of the past, Darwin began to speculate about the relationships among species. He realized that the "wonderful relationship in the same continent between the dead and the living" would throw light on the way in which species appeared and became extinct.

Stormy weather, treacherous currents, and bleak, unwelcoming shores of rock, ice, and rain-drenched forest make the passage around Tierra del Fuego one of the most difficult in the world. "The sight of such a coast," Darwin wrote, "is enough to make a landsman dream for a week about shipwrecks, peril, and death." The *Beagle* visited these dangerous waters several times, cruising the Beagle Channel, a waterway that had been named for the ship on an earlier voyage. Here Darwin saved a shore party from being stranded when he dashed into enormous waves to prevent their boats from being washed out to sea. FitzRoy gratefully named a nearby 7,000-foot peak Mount Darwin in his honor.

On an earlier visit to Tierra del Fuego, FitzRoy had picked up three Fuegian natives, whom he called York

Darwin published this drawing of a reconstructed skeleton of the Megatherium, or giant ground sloth, one of the many extinct creatures he unearthed from the plains of Argentina.

Minster (after a cathedral in England), Jemmy Button (FitzRoy had bought him from his mother for a large button), and Fuegia Basket (because she liked to carry a basket). FitzRoy had taken the Fuegians back to London, where they learned about various aspects of "civilized" life, such as Christianity, agriculture, clothing, and the use of spoons and forks. Now the *Beagle* was returning them to Tierra del Fuego, along with a young preacher from the Anglican Church's Missionary Society, to spread civilization among the Fuegians, whose culture was one of the least advanced on earth. But the captain's experiment failed miserably. The three "civilized" Fuegians promptly returned to their old way of life, and the young missionary demanded to be taken back aboard the *Beagle*. FitzRoy offered to take Jemmy Button back as well, but the Fuegian wanted to stay in his own country. When the *Beagle* sailed away at last from Tierra del Fuego, Darwin saw the smoke from Jemmy's signal fire, "a last and long farewell, as the ship stood on her course into the open sea."

The episode of the Fuegians was a sobering one for Darwin, who like most Europeans of his time firmly believed that the Western way of life was the most advanced. He decided that it was a mistake to think that "savages" should be "civilized" overnight. The Fuegians, the Aborigines of Australia, and other indigenous peoples should be left to work out their own destinies, Darwin concluded, but he correctly foresaw that the march of European colonialism and the modern economy would threaten their survival.

In June 1834 the *Beagle* reached the west coast of South America, where it spent more than a year. Darwin's main interest during this part of the voyage was geology, stimulated by the second volume of Lyell's *Principles of Geology*, which he had received by mail. Geological hammer in hand, Darwin studied the rock formations of the Andes, one of the earth's youngest and most rugged moun-

The Beagle's *Fuegian passengers, drawn by Captain FitzRoy: Fuegia Basket (top left), Jemmy Button (center left and right), and York Minster (bottom left and right). Darwin witnessed the failure of FitzRoy's attempt to force Western "civilization" upon these Fuegians.*

tain chains, marveling at a forest of petrified trees and a bed of fossil seashells 12,000 feet above sea level. He also saw volcanic explosions and survived an earthquake. Impressed by these dramatic proofs that the earth's surface is a shifting and ever-changing place, Darwin concluded that the physical conditions of life are fluid and changeable. His geological observations, along with his thoughts about the fossil species he had found—similar to and yet different

Concepcion, Chile, lay in ruins after an earth-quake in 1835. Darwin visited the ruins a few days later and called them "the most awful yet interesting spectacle I ever beheld."

from living creatures—helped shape his insight that life itself is fluid, ever changing in response to changes in its environment.

The South American coastal survey was the *Beagle's* primary mission. Once it was completed, the *Beagle* visited the Galápagos Islands for a month before heading west for the long voyage home in October 1835. The ship touched at Tahiti, New Zealand, Australia, and a number of smaller islands on its homeward journey, but these visits were brief and offered Darwin less scope for sustained exploration than he had enjoyed in South America. He made good use of his time, however, examining coral reefs and lagoons in the Pacific and Indian oceans, watching a pair of platypuses playing in a river in Australia, chipping samples from the volcanic slopes of Ascension Island in the Atlantic, and rambling around Napoleon Bonaparte's tomb on the lonely island of Saint Helena.

By this time, the voyage had lasted longer than anyone had expected, and Darwin and his shipmates were heartily eager to be home. They were cast into gloom by FitzRoy's announcement that, in order to complete a series of astronomical measurements around the world, the *Beagle* would cross the Atlantic and make a final stop in Brazil before returning to England. Upon learning of this delay, Darwin wrote peevishly to his sister Susan, "I loathe, I abhor the sea, & all ships which sail on it." But the ship spent only a few days in Brazil before turning toward England. Finally, as Darwin wrote, "On the 2nd of October we made the shores of England; and at Falmouth I left the *Beagle*, having lived aboard the good little vessel nearly five years."

The Birth of a Theory

As soon as the *Beagle* had docked at Falmouth in October of 1836, Darwin hastened home for a jubilant reunion with his family. Then he plunged into the long hard work of sorting out the products of his trip: a 770-page diary, lengthy notebooks on geology and zoology, and thousands of specimens of birds, plants, insects, and rocks. With his zoological specimens divided into groups—birds, insects, and so on—he decided to ask a top specialist in each category to classify and describe the material.

Darwin was able to enlist the help of some eminent naturalists because he had already become a bit of a celebrity. The fossils and other specimens he had sent to Henslow over the years had caused a sensation; in addition, Henslow had circulated some of Darwin's letters among fellow naturalists, and they had aroused much interest. The scientific community expected great things from Darwin. Adam Sedgwick had told the headmaster of Darwin's old school in Shrewsbury that Darwin would become "a great name among the Naturalists of Europe"—a comment that vastly pleased Dr. Robert when he learned of it. And geologist Charles Lyell, who met Darwin upon his return and quickly became a lifelong friend, was so impressed with the young naturalist's work that he arranged for Darwin to join the Geological Society of London. In the years immediately following his voyage, Darwin delivered many scientific papers to meetings of the society (despite the sickening stage fright he always felt during public appearances) and he served as its secretary.

It soon became clear that preparing the results of the voyage for publication would take a lot of time. It was equally clear that Charles Darwin had finally found his true direction in life. His plans to enter the church were quietly dropped, and Dr. Robert provided his son with a comfortable income so that he could devote his full attention to natural history. Darwin also received a government grant toward the cost of publishing a huge book called The Zoology of the Voyage of H.M.S. Beagle; Darwin was to edit the five volumes, which would be written by the naturalists who were working on his collections. In addition, Darwin wanted to write a book about his experiences during the voyage. After a few months spent in Shrewsbury and Cambridge, he rented rooms in London so that he could be near the scientific societies and his fellow naturalists, and set to work.

Charles Lyell, founder of the science of geology, was one of Darwin's inspirations; Lyell's failure to support Darwin's ideas publicly would be one of Darwin's greatest disappointments.

Darwin hated London, a city so darkened by soot, grime, and fog that it seemed to be in mourning for "the death of the sun," as he complained. Still, the city's intellectual life sparkled. Through his brother, Ras, and his new friend Lyell, Darwin received invitations to parties at the home of the celebrated mathematician Charles Babbage, where the scientific elite mingled with fashionable ladies and such prominent writers as historian Thomas Carlyle.

Despite his absorbing workload and his busy social life, Darwin began to feel lonely. By 1838 he was contemplating a new adventure: marriage. He drew up a list of the advan-

Emma Wedgwood was a loving and devoted wife to Darwin, although she had little interest in science and was disturbed by some of Darwin's ideas.

tages and disadvantages of matrimony. The advantages included children, someone to take care of the house, and companionship—"better than a dog anyhow." The disadvantages included "less money for books" and, most terrifying, "loss of time." In the end, the advantages outweighed the disadvantages, and Darwin began courting his cousin Emma Wedgwood. She accepted his proposal, and they were married in January 1839.

Darwin's decision to marry may seem rather cold-blooded, but there is no doubt that he and Emma loved each other and were very happy together. They were well suited to one another: Darwin needed someone to take care of him, and Emma was a cheerful, affectionate woman who enjoyed pampering her husband. Their union was one of several marriages between Darwin and Wedgwood cousins that further linked the two families. Josiah Wedgwood II gave the couple a handsome sum upon their marriage; together with the money from Robert Darwin, this settlement ensured the financial comfort of Charles Darwin and his family. Not only was Darwin spared the necessity of working for his living, but his investments made him a rich man.

Charles and Emma's first home was a rented house in London. When they moved in, Darwin pronounced himself "astounded" at the bulk of his books, rocks, and other scientific clutter—Emma's reactions were not recorded. A few months later, Darwin's first book was published. It was his account of the *Beagle* voyage, issued as part of a three-volume set that also included books by FitzRoy and another *Beagle* officer. Darwin waited nervously to see how it would be received. He need not have worried. His book was hailed as the best written and most interesting of the three. Lyell and other scientists applauded it, and Darwin's hero, Alexander von Humboldt, said that it was one of the best travel books ever published. Darwin's book sold well and was later reissued on its own under several titles, including

Journal of Researches and *The Voyage of the Beagle*. Darwin was thrilled to discover that he could write, and write well. He wrote to Henslow, "If I live to be eighty years old I shall not cease to marvel at finding myself an author," and added, "This marvellous transformation is all owing to you."

Charles and Emma Darwin's first child, William Erasmus, was born in December 1839. Darwin feared for Emma's safety, for many women died in childbirth in the 19th century, but he later rejoiced in his healthy son. Typically, Darwin observed the infant with the same care he devoted to a new species, peering into William's crib and filling pages with notes on the baby's facial expressions, which he compared with those of Jenny, an orangutan in the London zoo. The similarities, he found, were fascinating. This was the beginning of Darwin's lifelong interest in the facial expressions and emotions of both people and animals.

Around this time Darwin's health broke down. For months he suffered from piercing headaches, stomach pains, prolonged vomiting, painful skin rashes, trembling and pains around the heart, and an overall feeling of weakness. Over the next 25 years or so, he would repeatedly be plagued with ill health and fatigue. During much of that time, he would be able to work for only a few hours a day, and there were several periods when his health worsened and he could not work at all for months on end. The sportsman of Darwin's youth, the adventurer who had

Darwin was photographed with William, his eldest child, in 1842. Several years earlier, Darwin had suffered the first of the severe breakdowns in his health that were to trouble him for the rest of his life.

galloped fearlessly over the pampas of Argentina and crossed the Andes Mountains, became a chronic invalid who feared that an overnight visit to friends would exhaust his strength and make him ill.

The nature of Darwin's illness has been the subject of much speculation. No doctor during Darwin's lifetime— not even his father—could pin down just what the trouble was. In the years since his death, researchers have offered many diagnoses based on the symptoms that Darwin recorded. For a time everyone assumed that he had been infected with some debilitating tropical disease in South America. He is known to have been bitten by an insect that sometimes carries Chagas' disease, a tropical illness that produces a high fever and attacks the liver and other organs. Yet Darwin's symptoms do not precisely match the classic symptoms of Chagas' disease, although some medical specialists feel that he may have had a mild version of the condition. Unlike most victims of serious tropical diseases, Darwin lived to the ripe old age of 73, and his health was better during the last decade of his life than it had been for many years.

Some recent scholars believe that Darwin's illness was the result of psychological disturbance rather than organic disease. A New York psychiatrist named Ralph Colp Jr. spent years studying the accounts of Darwin's illness. In his 1977 book *To Be an Invalid: The Illness of Charles Darwin,* Colp suggested that Darwin's physical symptoms were signs of an inner conflict about his ideas of evolution. On one hand, Darwin was convinced that his theories were true; but on the other, he dreaded the scorn and outrage that would be directed at him for contradicting the established view of life. The tension between these two powerful feelings, Colp believed, made Darwin ill. British psychologist John Bowlby agreed with Colp that Darwin's illness was psychological in origin, but he felt that its cause was childhood emotional trauma—chiefly the death of Darwin's mother and the grief that young Charles never outwardly expressed. In his book *Charles Darwin: A New Life* (1990), Bowlby described a medical condition known as hyperventilation syndrome, which is connected with emotional stress; its symptoms are similar to Darwin's. Both Colp and Bowlby felt that Darwin's occasional long spells of anxiety, weakness, and stomach trouble were triggered by crises in his family or professional life.

No diagnosis of a man long dead can ever be more than tentative. Many experts now agree, however, that Darwin's illness could have been caused by a combination of organic and psychological disorders, in which some disease—probably contracted in the tropics—interacted with stress and anxiety. Whatever their origin, Darwin's recurrent symptoms were very real, and he bitterly regretted the time lost from his work whenever he was sick.

In 1842 Darwin bought a country estate called Down House in the rural village of Downe, outside London, in the county of Kent. Darwin loved his new home, where he was surrounded by trees and flowers instead of streets and soot. He fitted out one large room as his study and proceeded to cram it with books, notes on work in progress, and piles of correspondence. The house was large enough to hold a staff of servants as well as Darwin's growing family. By 1856, he and Emma had had 10 children: William, Anne (Annie), Mary, Henrietta (Etty), George, Elizabeth (Bessy), Francis, Leonard, Horace, and Charles. Mary and Charles died in infancy; Annie died at the age of 10 after a serious illness, a tragedy that haunted Darwin ever after.

Life at Down House quickly fell into a tranquil routine that Darwin followed, with few exceptions, for the rest of his life. He started the day with a walk on the Sandwalk, a sandy path he had constructed around a grove of trees on the estate grounds. After breakfast he wrote in his study from 8:00 until 9:30, and then he read the day's mail. At 10:30 he went back to work for an hour or so before

Down House, in a country village, was Darwin's much-loved refuge from the soot and noise of London. As the years passed, Darwin grew less and less willing to leave the familiar comforts of home.

another spin around the Sandwalk. At this time he sometimes took a cold outdoor shower, which he believed to be good for his health.

After the midday meal he read the newspaper and wrote letters in the drawing room. At 3:00 he rested in his bedroom for an hour; Emma frequently read novels aloud to him at that time. Late in the afternoon Darwin took another walk and then worked for another hour. While his children were growing up, he often took unscheduled breaks to romp in the garden with them.

After a light evening meal, he liked to play backgammon with Emma. (The care with which he kept a tally of their scores reflects his passion for collecting and recording facts: In 1876 he informed his friend Asa Gray, an American botanist, that he had won 2,795 games and Emma 2,490.) After reading a scientific book for an hour or two, Darwin went to bed at 10:30.

Darwin made occasional visits to health resorts or to see Ras in London. As time went on, he left Down House less and less often, but he had many visitors. Some were family members, but others were Darwin's scientific friends—Henslow, Lyell, and others. One welcome guest was Joseph Hooker (1817–1911), a botanist whom Darwin had met in 1839. Later, Hooker recalled his first impression of Darwin: "a rather tall and rather broad-shouldered man, with a slight stoop, an agreeable and animated expression when talking, beetle brows, and a hollow but mellow voice." Hooker admired Darwin and dreamed of making voyages of scientific exploration like the one Darwin had made in the *Beagle*; eventually he traveled to Antarctica and the Himalaya Mountains. Hooker became Darwin's closest confidant and was to emerge as one of the staunchest supporters of Darwin's ideas. In 1850 Darwin became acquainted with a young zoologist named Thomas Henry Huxley (1825–95), who had just returned from a round-the-world voyage much like the *Beagle*'s. Like Hooker, Huxley became Darwin's close friend, frequent visitor, and fervent supporter.

The five volumes on the *Beagle* zoology, with notes and other material by Darwin, were published between 1839 and 1843. By the time they were finished, Darwin had not only written his book about the *Beagle* journey but had also begun writing a three-volume study called *The Geology of the Voyage of H.M.S. Beagle*. The first installment was a book on coral reefs, published in 1842, in which Darwin advanced a theory about how coral reefs are formed. Drawing on his studies of corals in Tahiti and various Indian Ocean islands, he explained that the tiny living creatures called coral polyps, which can live only in warm, shallow water, keep building new coral colonies on top of old ones as the sea bed very slowly sinks. In this way, coral reefs can rise from great depths to form rings, called atolls, on top of sinking volcanic cones; the reefs are dead at the bot-

Botanist Joseph Hooker was a frequent visitor at Down House. It was to Hooker that Darwin first revealed the details of his theory of evolution.

tom and alive only at the very top. Darwin's insights into the way reefs are formed are still recognized as fundamentally correct. The other two geological volumes dealt with volcanic islands (1844) and the geology of South America (1846). All three won high praise from Lyell and other scientists, both for the quality of Darwin's observations and ideas and for the style with which he expressed them.

In October 1846, with the geological series completed, Darwin wrote to his old mentor Henslow, "You cannot think how delighted I am at having finished all my *Beagle* materials." It had taken Darwin a decade to publish the results of the five-year voyage. Yet in truth Darwin would never be completely finished with his "*Beagle* materials." His major work lay ahead, and for years to come he would grapple with scientific problems that had their origin in his voyage of discovery.

After the *Beagle* voyage, Darwin never left England again. Though many 19th-century naturalists made arduous field trips to the most remote and dangerous corners of the earth, Darwin settled into a life of domestic comfort, quiet contemplation, and writing. But during these years he made a second journey, more challenging than the first—a mental journey that carried him beyond the frontier of knowledge into new, uncharted territory. For in 1837, while he was still sorting his collections and writing his account of the voyage, he had begun working privately on a subject that came to occupy more and more of his thoughts—a subject that he called the transmutation, or change, of species.

When Darwin began to think seriously about the origin of species, he was already half-convinced of the reality of evolution. He was familiar with the arguments of scientists—such as his grandfather Erasmus Darwin and the French thinker Lamarck—who claimed that species were not fixed but rather changed over time. Darwin now knew of several facts that supported this claim. One such fact was the fossil record, with its evidence of extinct creatures. Darwin's own discoveries in South America had pointed up the similarities between extinct and living species, which suggested that the living were descendants of the extinct. Another well-known fact that argued in favor of evolution was the presence of rudimentary, seemingly useless organs in some living creatures, such as the small, nonfunctional wings of ostriches and other flightless birds and the leg bones found inside the bodies of certain snakes. Darwin came to see these useless structures as signs that these birds and snakes had descended from ancestral species that had once flown on wings and walked on legs.

As early as 1836, while homeward bound from the Galápagos, Darwin was thinking about what the vice-governor of the islands had told him: that the tortoises' shell patterns varied from island to island. Such variations, he wrote in his shipboard notebook, "would undermine the stability of Species." Soon he was to see more evidence of such variations.

The birds of the Galápagos Islands played a crucial part in Darwin's views on the evolution of species, or, as he called it, "descent with modification." Yet he did not recognize their significance until after he had turned his specimens over to ornithologist John Gould of the Zoological Society of London. Darwin's collection of Galápagos birds included 4 species of mockingbirds and 13 species of small birds called finches. Darwin did not even realize that all the finches were finches—they looked so different from the finches he knew that he thought some of them were wrens, blackbirds, and other kinds of birds. He was astonished when Gould told him in March 1837 that the mockingbird

The quiet room where the evolution revolution occurred: Darwin's study at Down House. Files are stacked on one side of the fireplace; the curtain on the other side conceals a bathroom.

species were very closely related and that a dozen or so other specimens were actually different kinds of finches, related to one another yet distinct from all other known finches. Could the different types have branched out from common ancestors? Were the mockingbird varieties all descended from one kind of mockingbird, and the finch varieties from one kind of finch?

Darwin studied the finches, cursing himself for not having kept better records of where each specimen came from. Working from memory and from his own notes and those of others aboard the *Beagle* who had helped with the collecting, he established that the different species came from different islands. Clearly, geographic separation had something to do with variation. Darwin concluded that all the finches had descended from a single parent species that reached the islands from the South American mainland. Over many generations, the original finch was modified into a dozen new varieties to suit the islands' various ecological niches. One species had a long, sharp beak for pricking seabirds to drink their blood; another had a short, thick beak for cracking seeds; a third had a sturdy beak for overturning pebbles to find food; a fourth had a narrow, curved beak for plucking insects from cacti, and so on. Darwin was becoming convinced that life had adapted in response to the shaping power of environment and necessity. In July 1837, four months after his meeting with Gould, he started his first notebook on transmutation, or evolution.

Scholars are still tracing the influences that stimulated Darwin and are still working out the precise timetable of his ideas and statements about evolutionary theory. But his notes, letters, and autobiography show that by mid-1837 he was convinced that species change; as he wrote in his notebook, some natural law or force must "alter the race to [fit a] changing world." But what was that law? What mechanism allowed transmutation to take place? Darwin began a systematic collection of what he later called "all facts which bore in any way on the variation of animals and plants."

In his ambitious and wide-ranging quest for information, Darwin was like someone assembling a jigsaw puzzle. He knew what the finished picture was supposed to represent: the plants and animals of the modern world. But he did not know how many puzzle pieces it would take to explain how these plants and animals were formed and distributed across the earth, or how fossils fit into the picture. He gathered his puzzle pieces—facts and specimens—from far and wide and patiently fitted them together. Some of the pieces came from the scores of travel books and scientific journals through which he sifted, but most came by mail. He sent out hundreds of letters to travelers and

The large ground finch of the Galápagos Islands. The Galápagos finches were a key piece in the puzzle of evolution, although Darwin did not realize their significance until after he had returned to England.

scientists requesting all kinds of information about varieties and species; some of the letters contained detailed and lengthy questionnaires. This voluminous correspondence on the topic was to continue for years, long after Darwin had published his views on the origin of species. He knew that in science a theory must be tested by its ability to explain multitudes of minute facts, and he never tired of collecting those facts.

One area of inquiry concerned the distribution, or geographic range, of species. Darwin's observations in the Galápagos, Australia, and elsewhere had shown him that islands have a high percentage of endemic, or naturally occurring, species that occur nowhere else. He reasoned that new species are more likely to split off among small, isolated populations of plants and animals that cannot breed with the larger parent populations. Islands offer perfect conditions for the formation of new species. On islands, plants and animals are cut off from their parent stocks on the closest continents. They gradually diverge until they form completely new species, as the finches of the Galápagos had diverged from the ancestral South American finch. How, though, did the ancestral organisms get to islands like the Galápagos in the first place?

Darwin avidly collected information about species transmission. He asked hunters how far birds could fly. He wrote to a sailor who had once been shipwrecked on a remote island to ask what species of trees the castaway had noticed among the driftwood on the beach. Later, at Down House, Darwin conducted experiments to test his ideas about how plants spread from continents to islands. He soaked seeds in jars of salt water and then planted them, reporting with glee that carrot seeds had sprouted after 42 days "at sea." The British consul in Norway sent Darwin tropical seed pods that had drifted for thousands of miles on the Gulf Stream, and he got those to sprout, too. He sprouted grass seeds from bird droppings and from the mud on partridges' feet. At times every shelf in Darwin's study was lined with his soaking jars and sprouting pots. Changing the water in the jars became such a nuisance that Darwin was glad when his children could lend a hand. Darwin also speculated that lizards and other small animals could be carried to islands by birds of prey or on floating trees, and although he did not put these notions to the test, he collected stories about creatures found by travelers in unexpected places.

Domesticated plants and animals formed another very important subject of Darwin's quest. He was well aware that many varieties of plants and animals had been created through controlled breeding; for example, by mating their largest bulls and cows, stock farmers would eventually produce a breed of larger cattle. Darwin knew that a variety is not the same thing as a species; a stock breeder can create a new variety of cattle, but that variety can still interbreed with other cattle, if allowed to do so. No plant or animal breeder had yet produced an entirely separate species. Darwin believed that it would take a long time—tens of thousands of years, perhaps, or even more—for a new species to separate completely from the parent species. It seemed logical to him that if stock breeders continued to mate their cattle selectively over such a long period of time, the new breed would ultimately become a distinct species, apart from all other cattle.

Fascinated by the way in which domesticated plants and animals were constantly being transformed by controlled breeding, Darwin attended livestock shows and subscribed to seed catalogues. He became particularly interested in the popular pastime of raising pigeons for racing or show, and he studied how pigeon fanciers bred their birds to accentuate certain characteristics such as fan-shaped tails or fluffy topknots. Later Darwin raised pigeons at Down House so that he could observe the results of selective breeding at first hand. He made many friends in the down-to-earth world of the pigeon fanciers. To these humble folk, Darwin was not a prestigious scientist but rather a genial country squire and fellow bird enthusiast.

Although Darwin's search for facts about the species question lasted for the rest of his life, his basic notions about the origin of species came together within little more than a year. His first transmutation notebook was filled by February 1838; several more followed later that year. By this time, Darwin knew that species evolved. Now he wanted to know *why* and *how* they evolved. He was aware that members of the same species differ from one another in countless small ways. A single litter might contain three black puppies and one brown one; a single clutch of pigeon eggs could produce one hatchling with slightly narrower wings than the others. Nature, Darwin reflected, constantly produced these random variations. In the case of domestic animals, a breeder might select a particular variation and then control the puppy's or the pigeon's mating to emphasize that trait. But what force acted upon wild plants and animals? Why did some variations become established as new species?

A crucial piece of the puzzle fell into place in the fall of 1838. Darwin read "for amusement" a book called *Essay on the Principle of Population* (1798) by the British clergyman and economist Thomas Malthus, who had set out to investigate the causes of human misery in the squalid, overcrowded slums of London and other cities. Malthus pointed out that nearly all species produce far more offspring than can possibly survive, a fact long known to naturalists. Most of these offspring, however, die before they can reproduce—if this were not true, the earth would soon be covered many layers deep with the offspring of a single prolific creature such as the tapeworm (which lays 60 million eggs each year). Malthus then argued that populations grow faster than their food supply can increase. In other words, nature's great fertility produces more organisms than its resources can support. Without some limit or check on fertility, population growth would soon outgrow the resources necessary for survival. The necessary check on this growth is provided by the constant struggle for food and other resources. Life is a competition for resources in which many organisms inevitably perish at a very young age.

Malthus was mainly concerned with the human condition. Fearing that unchecked population growth would lead to a ruthless struggle for survival, he advised against reforms to aid the poor, claiming that making poor people less miserable would only encourage them to have more children, which in the end would make their living conditions even *more* miserable. Darwin, though tenderhearted, subscribed to this cold-blooded view of human well-being. More important for his scientific work, he instantly saw that Malthus's argument made a great deal of sense as applied to the world of plants and animals.

Mathematically speaking, Malthus was right: Unchecked reproduction causes populations to outgrow their food sources. There are not enough resources to go around, and in that sense, life is a constant struggle to survive. Here was the force Darwin had been seeking, the unseen principle that "selected" some creatures to die and others to live and reproduce.

Combining the idea of struggle with the fact of constant variations in nature, Darwin realized that some individuals would be born with variations that would give them an advantage—a hawk that could fly a little faster than other hawks, a cedar tree that grew a little taller than other cedars and thus received more sunlight, a finch with a slightly thicker beak that could crack open hard seeds. Because of these advantages, these individuals would probably live longer and produce more offspring than their siblings. Their offspring would inherit the favorable characteristics and in turn pass them on to future generations (it was well known that parents' traits were inherited by their offspring, although no one yet knew just how heredity worked).

The crowded, squalid slums of 19th-century London inspired economist Thomas Malthus to investigate the question of population growth. Malthus's work gave Darwin another piece of the evolution puzzle.

Thus, over many generations, the sturdy-billed finches or the taller cedars would be established first as a variety and then as an independent species, either replacing the parent species or moving into a different ecological niche. To this shaping force Darwin gave the name "natural selection," in contrast to the "artifical selection" practiced by plant and animal breeders.

By the end of 1838, Darwin had arrived at the core of his great achievement—his theory of evolution and its operating mechanism, natural selection. Darwin's insight was rooted in a cluster of interrelated facts, ideas, and observations:

• Earth's history stretches back millions of years (demonstrated by Charles Lyell and others; supported by Darwin's field geology).

• Species are mutable, or subject to change (suggested by Erasmus Darwin and other earlier thinkers; confirmed by evidence of links between extinct and living species and by production of new domestic varieties).

• Variations occur when populations are isolated from parent species (Galápagos birds).

• Global and local environments change continuously; life must adapt to changing conditions (geological and fossil evidence).

• Individual organisms are born with subtle variations (common knowledge; confirmed by plant and animal breeders).

• Organisms' characteristics are inherited by their offspring (common knowledge; confirmed by plant and animal breeders).

• Life is a struggle for survival (Malthus).

• Variations that help organisms survive and adapt are passed on, and eventually new species evolve through natural selection (Darwin).

Darwin did not rush to announce his grand new insight. Instead, he quietly continued to gather facts about species while he carried on with his work on the zoology and geology of the *Beagle*, married Emma, and settled at Down House. Darwin's correspondents and scientific acquaintances were aware that he was making a study of species, but they did not know how firmly he was convinced that species are mutable, or that he had come up with a theory to explain how new species are formed. For the time being, Darwin kept his ideas a secret.

5

A "Devil's Chaplain"

In 1842, Darwin wrote out a 35-page summary of his thoughts on evolution and natural selection. Two years later, he prepared a more detailed version that ran to 231 pages. The 1844 manuscript was in two parts. In the first part, Darwin discussed variations among both domestic and wild organisms and described how natural selection works; in the second part, he reviewed the arguments for and against natural selection. Darwin was not yet ready to publish his theory, but he knew that his work represented what he called "a considerable step in science," and he did not want it to be lost. He left instructions with Emma: In case of his sudden death, she was to give the species manuscript to one of his scientific colleagues to carry on the work. Darwin suggested that Lyell, Henslow, or Hooker would be a good choice. It was the last of these, the young botanist Hooker, to whom Darwin finally unveiled his species theory.

In January 1844 Darwin wrote to Hooker, who had just returned from a voyage to Antarctica, that he had been gathering facts for "a very presumptuous work." He went on to say that "gleams of light have come, & I am almost convinced (quite contrary to the opinion I started with)

Charles Darwin in 1851. Darwin's books about the natural history of the Beagle voyage had established him as a scientist, but he was still nearly a decade away from publishing his radical ideas about evolution and natural selection.

that species are not (it is like confessing a murder) immutable. . . . I think I have found out (here's presumption!) the simple way by which species become exquisitely adapted to various ends." Later, Darwin sent Hooker the 231-page "sketch" of his theory. Hooker was dubious at first. Like most scientists and nonscientists, he had assumed that species are immutable, or unchanging. But a careful reading of the manuscript, along with many long talks with Darwin in the months and years that followed, eventually convinced Hooker that Darwin was right.

Even after converting Hooker to evolution, Darwin held back from publishing his theory. In fact, he did not publish his ideas about evolution and natural selection until 1859, 20 years after he had formulated them. The central mystery of Darwin's career thus becomes: Why did he wait so long to go public with his evolutionary theories?

Vestiges of Creation, a book about species evolution, caused an uproar in the 1840s. The author published Vestiges *anonymously, knowing that it would be controversial. Darwin dreaded being at the center of a similar controversy.*

One clue lies in the fate of a book called Vestiges of Creation, published anonymously in 1844 by an Edinburgh bookseller named Robert Chambers (1802–83). Vestiges contained a fair amount of sloppy or inaccurate science, but, more important, it expressed the view that the universe—including all species of living things—had evolved according to natural laws. The author of Vestiges did not say how or why evolution had occurred, only that it had occurred. He claimed that all life was interrelated, that new species arose through natural processes, not by acts of divine creation, and that species

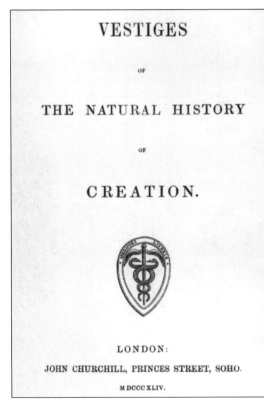

VESTIGES

OF

THE NATURAL HISTORY

OF

CREATION.

LONDON:
JOHN CHURCHILL, PRINCES STREET, SOHO.
M DCCC XLIV.

changed over time. These claims made the book so controversial that for the rest of his life Robert Chambers refused to acknowledge publicly that he had written it; the identity of "Mr. Vestiges" was a popular guessing game at intellectual dinner parties, although eventually a number of people came to know or suspect Chambers's authorship. *Vestiges* did not deny the role of God in guiding the evolutionary progress—indeed, its tone was respectful toward religion—but the church and mainstream scientists heaped scorn and abuse on the book because it threatened the biblical view of life.

The idea of evolution did more than simply contradict the Bible's story of creation. It raised the specter of materialism, which was deeply disturbing to Victorian society. To many people, materialism—the belief that the workings of the universe can be explained in terms of matter and natural laws—meant that God's existence could no longer be regarded as necessary and unquestionable.

Although many people had no difficulty in believing in both God and evolution, others found their faith shaken. One of the latter was the poet Alfred Lord Tennyson. In 1850 he published a long poem called "In Memoriam," which became one of the most popular poems of the Victorian era. In the poem, which was partly inspired by *Vestiges of Creation,* Tennyson mourned the death of a friend. To create a mood of despair, he used images drawn from natural history and from the debate over evolution to underline the heartlessness of the natural world. The poem's best-known image is "Nature, red in tooth and claw"—a catchphrase that many people later adopted as a summary of Darwin's "struggle for existence." Tennyson also wrote plaintively of fossils buried in cliffs, with Nature ruthlessly crying out, "A thousand types are gone: I care for nothing, all shall go." Yet despite these bleak images, "In Memoriam" is in some ways pro-evolution, for in the course of the poem the author finds comfort in picturing his dead friend as an example of the superior beings into which humans may one day develop through a form of spiritual evolution.

The agitation over *Vestiges* made it clear to Darwin that his own much more detailed theory of evolution was sure to set off a storm of controversy. By nature gentle and retiring, Darwin shrank from the thought of becoming a public spectacle. He also shrank from causing pain to his loved ones, particularly to Emma, who in the early days of their marriage had fretted that Darwin's unorthodox ideas would keep him out of heaven. She had written him a touching letter about her fears that they would be separated for eternity; Darwin kept this letter close, and he later noted on it that he had kissed and cried over it many times. But Darwin's own Christianity, never very deeply held, gradually eroded as he worked out his theory of natural selection; the remnants of his faith were wiped out entirely by the suffering and death of his daughter Annie in 1851. Later in life he described himself as an agnostic—one who questions but does not flatly deny the existence of God. Although Emma remained a churchgoer and a believer until the end of her days, she also came to tolerate and even support her husband's work—without pretending, however, to take much interest in its details.

In addition to his dread of controversy, Darwin had scientific excuses for delaying the publication of his theory. The very fact that his ideas were controversial meant that they must rest on a sturdy foundation of evidence. Darwin felt that he needed more time to marshal still more facts and examples to support his case, for he wanted to anticipate every possible objection and defeat it before it could arise. So in 1846, when he finished his last geological book, he did not begin writing a book about evolution, although he continued to collect information for the book he planned to write one day on the subject. For the immediate future, he decided, he would take up a new project: the detailed examination of one particular group of organisms. He was pushed in this direction by Hooker, who reminded Darwin that biologists were expected to demonstrate their expertise by making a thorough study of a group of closely related species. Darwin decided that his evolutionary theory would be more likely to win acceptance if he first proved himself as an anatomist and a serious biologist, not merely a collector and observer. Perhaps, as some biographers have suggested, he was happy to postpone the evolution controversy a little longer. At any rate, the research project he began in 1846 taught him a great deal about relationships among species.

Annie Darwin, Charles and Emma's eldest daughter, died at the age of 10. Her death destroyed the last lingering remnants of Darwin's Christianity.

The subject of Darwin's close study was to be barnacles, sea-dwelling crustaceans whose hard shells accumulate in clusters on rocks, pilings, and other underwater surfaces—including the hulls of boats, where their thick encrustations slow the vessels' passage through the water. Darwin had brought back several interesting specimens of barnacles from the *Beagle* voyage, and he was eager to dissect and describe them. As often happened with Darwin, however, the project mushroomed into something much larger than he had envisioned. In his earnest desire to be thorough, he wound up devoting eight years to the study of barnacles, swapping specimens through the mail with other naturalists, dissecting and sketching, describing more species of barnacles than he had dreamed existed. Darwin's children grew up in a barnacle-filled household; one of them was overheard asking a playmate, "Where does your father work on *his* barnacles?"

Joseph Hooker later told Francis Darwin that Francis's

Some of the many anatomical drawings that Darwin produced during his eight-year study of barnacles. Some historians have viewed the barnacle project as Darwin's way of postponing the turmoil that publication of his evolutionary theories would cause.

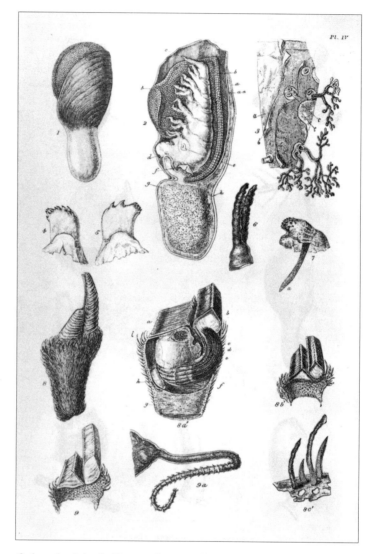

father had had "barnacles on the brain" for a long time before starting the project, and Darwin's letters and notes from the late 1840s contain frequent references to "my beloved Barnacles." Yet as the years dragged on, the little crustaceans lost some of their allure. Darwin started calling them "these everlasting Barnacles." In 1852 he joked to his cousin William Darwin Fox, "I hate a Barnacle as no man ever did before, not even a sailor in a slow-moving ship." Finally, in 1855, the immense project was completed.

Darwin published four large volumes on living and fossil barnacle species and was immediately recognized as the world's leading authority on the subject. His books on barnacles are still regarded as primary works in the field.

The barnacle years were eventful ones for Darwin and his family. Some incidents of the period were joyous: Darwin's new friendship with Thomas H. Huxley, for example, and the medal awarded him by the Royal Society in 1853 for his contributions to natural history. Some, such as the deaths of Darwin's father in 1848 and his daughter Annie's death a few years later, were tragic. Distress over Dr. Robert's illness and death may have contributed to a breakdown in Darwin's health that kept him bedridden for months during 1848 and 1849. Barely had Darwin recovered from his grief over his father's death when Annie, his beloved daughter, fell ill with a stomach complaint that caused prolonged vomiting. Darwin took her to a health resort to consult the best doctor he could find, but nothing helped. Annie grew weaker and weaker. From her bedside Darwin wrote tearfully to Emma, who was at home caring for the younger children, "I wish you could see her now, the perfection of gentleness, patience & gratitude—thankful til it is truly painful to hear her.—poor dear little soul." After a long decline, Annie died in the spring of 1851, leaving Darwin sick with sorrow over what he called "our bitter & cruel loss." A few weeks after Annie's death, Darwin wrote, "Oh that she could now know how deeply, how tenderly we do still & shall ever love her dear joyous face."

Through illness, the distractions of family life, and the demands of the "beloved Barnacles," Darwin had continued to work on his evolutionary material, gathering and sorting facts. Once his barnacle survey was complete, his friends Lyell and Hooker urged him to publish his work on the evolution of species, and Darwin agreed that the time had come. In 1856, with his 1844 manuscript in front of him and piles of notes on all sides, he began writing a book about his theory of "descent with modification" through natural selection. He knew that it would be his major contribution to science, and he expected to spend many years on the writing.

By this time, Darwin's colleagues knew that he was working on the topic of species and variation, but the details of his theory were known only to a few: Hooker, the American botanist Asa Gray, Darwin's brother Ras, and Lyell. Yet Darwin was not working in a vacuum. *Vestiges of Creation* had stirred up public debate on the idea of evolution, which was beginning to attract supporters. In 1852, a British philosopher named Herbert Spencer (1820–1903) argued in a magazine article that species had evolved, although he did not attempt to describe *how* they had evolved.

Alfred Russel Wallace, one of Darwin's colleagues in natural history, plunged Darwin into a professional dilemma by arriving independently at the theory of natural selection just as Darwin was preparing to publish his own ideas.

Meanwhile, on the other side of the world, another naturalist was working on the topic of species formation. He was Alfred Russel Wallace (1823–1913), whose interest in evolution had been aroused by *Vestiges of Creation*. During an expedition to the Amazon rain forest (1848–52), he had begun examining the evidence for the evolution of new species. In 1854 Wallace set off on an eight-year expedition to Indonesia and Malaysia, where he continued to ponder the species question. The following year he published an article called "On the Law which has Regulated the Introduction of New Species," in which he argued that every new species comes into being in the vicinity of "a pre-existing, closely allied species." Wallace was clearly working on the question of the evolution of species, although his article contained no hint of a method by which evolution could occur. Still, the appearance of the article prodded Darwin into starting his own book on evolution at last. He wrote to Wallace, congratulating him on the article and adding that he had been working on the species question for years and was writing a book on the subject.

By June of 1858, Darwin had written hundreds of pages of the book he planned to call *Natural Selection,* but huge chunks of this "everlasting species-Book," as he told Lyell, remained to be written. That month, Darwin received a parcel from Ternate, one of the Moluccas Islands in what is now Indonesia. The package was from Wallace and contained the manuscript of an article. Wallace had sent the article to Darwin, whom he respected, because he wanted Darwin's opinion of his new idea; he also asked Darwin to pass the manuscript along to Lyell. Darwin read the article and sat back appalled. Wallace had neatly summarized much of the theory of natural selection upon which Darwin had been laboring for 20 years.

Darwin now found himself in a dreadful dilemma. He was a fair man and had no wish to rob Wallace, who trusted him, of the credit for arriving at the theory of natural selection. At the same time, however, Darwin *had* formulated the theory years earlier, as some of his friends knew, and he had an understandable desire to receive the credit for his own work. He reproached himself for waiting so long to announce his theory; perhaps now his long years of effort were in vain.

He asked Lyell, who not only knew of Darwin's work but was one of the most respected scientists of the day, what he should do. Above all, he did not want Wallace to think him petty or greedy for fame. "I would far rather burn my whole book," he said, "than that he or any man should think that I had behaved in a paltry spirit." Lyell and Hooker came up with a plan to which Darwin agreed. They arranged to have the Darwin-Wallace theory presented at the July meeting of the Linnean Society, a natural history association in London. The presentation was made by the society's secretary and consisted of parts of Darwin's 1844 manuscript on natural selection, part of a letter Darwin had written to Asa Gray on the subject in 1857, and Wallace's paper from Ternate. The theory of natural selection had finally come before the world, and Darwin and Wallace were officially established as its co-authors, although the sequence of dates made it clear that Darwin had thought of it first.

The arrangement by which Darwin and Wallace shared the credit for discovering natural selection has often been hailed as a shining example of selfless cooperation and goodwill between scientists. In truth, Wallace was given no chance to agree to the plan. He was not even asked; it would have taken months for a letter to reach Ternate and for Wallace's answer to come back. Wallace did not even know about the joint presentation to the Linnean Society until three months after the meeting. To Darwin's great relief, Wallace claimed to be perfectly satisfied with the way the problem had been handled. He and Darwin were friends as well as colleagues to the end of Darwin's life, although they disagreed on some important scientific issues. Wallace had been led to natural selection by his observations of thousands of species in the wild, each perfectly fitted into its ecological niche, and by the recognition that existence is a struggle for survival (which, like Darwin, he had absorbed from Malthus's *Essay on Population*). He knew that he and Darwin had come up with the idea of natural selection independently—there was never any question of Darwin pirating Wallace's idea—and he accepted the fact that Darwin had reached it first. In both their private letters and their published works, each man spoke fondly and respectfully of the other. Wallace does not seem to have minded that it was Darwin's name, not his, that became firmly associated with their revolutionary insight.

Plagued with troubles and sorrow, Darwin did not attend the Linnean Society meeting at which the theory was presented. His youngest child, Charles, had just died of scarlet fever, and his daughter Etty was sick. Nevertheless,

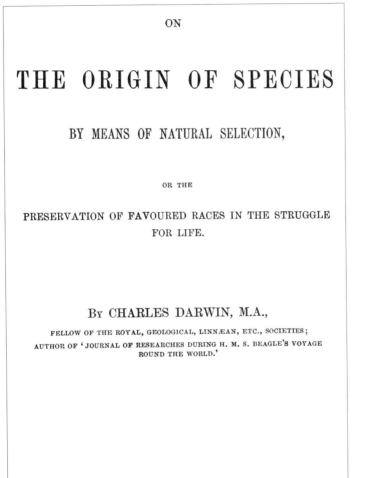

ON

THE ORIGIN OF SPECIES

BY MEANS OF NATURAL SELECTION,

OR THE

PRESERVATION OF FAVOURED RACES IN THE STRUGGLE FOR LIFE.

By CHARLES DARWIN, M.A.,

FELLOW OF THE ROYAL, GEOLOGICAL, LINNÆAN, ETC., SOCIETIES ;
AUTHOR OF 'JOURNAL OF RESEARCHES DURING H. M. S. BEAGLE'S VOYAGE
ROUND THE WORLD.'

LONDON:
JOHN MURRAY, ALBEMARLE STREET.
1859.

In 1859, 20 years after developing the theory of evolution through natural selection, Darwin published his first book on the subject. As he had expected, the Origin *touched off a storm of controversy.*

he realized that he must now publish something on natural selection, and soon. He abandoned the big book at which he had been plugging away and hurriedly prepared a more concise treatment, which was published in November 1859 under the title *On the Origin of Species by Means of Natural Selection*. The subject had aroused so much interest that booksellers snapped up all 1,250 copies of the first edition on the day it was offered to the book trade.

Although the *Origin* was much shorter than the book Darwin had planned to write, it was still a substantial volume of more than 400 pages. In it, Darwin discussed subjects as diverse as pigeon breeders, fossil fish, Russian cockroaches, icebergs, and the subtle ecological relationship that links cats, mice, bees, and red clover. He drew upon 20 years of reading, observing, collecting, and experimenting in geology, anatomy, botany, and zoology to make two main points. The first point was that species evolve and are adapted to fit their circumstances. (Darwin was still using the term "descent with modification"; he did not use "evolution" until the sixth edition of the *Origin*, in 1872). The second point was that natural selection, which favors the organisms that are best equipped to survive and reproduce, is the primary mechanism by which new species are slowly formed:

> It may be said that natural selection is daily and hourly scrutinising, throughout the world, every variation, even the slightest; rejecting that which is bad, preserving and adding up all that is good; silently and insensibly working, whenever and wherever opportunity offers, at the improvement of each organic being in relation to its . . . conditions of life. We see nothing of these slow changes in progress, until the hand of time has marked the long lapses of ages, and then so imperfect is our view into long past geological ages, that we only see that the forms of life are now different from what they formerly were.

Darwin rightly called the *Origin* "one long argument" against miraculous divine creation. In the last chapter, he summed up the argument, closing with a paragraph that captures the sense of wonder that nature and its laws held for him. Darwin had no need to imagine supernatural mysteries—the earthly world before his eyes was enough to inspire awe:

> It is interesting to contemplate an entangled bank, clothed with many plants of many kinds, with birds singing on the bushes, with various insects flitting about, and with worms crawling through the damp earth, and to reflect that these elaborately constructed forms, so different from each other, and dependent on each other in so complex a manner, have all been produced by laws acting around us. . . . There is a grandeur in this view of life, with its several powers, having been originally breathed into a few forms or into one; and that, whilst this planet has gone cycling on according to the fixed law of gravity, from so simple a beginning endless forms most beautiful and wonderful have been, and are being, evolved.

As Darwin had expected, *On the Origin of Species* touched off a heated debate among both scientists and the general public. He was heartened by the reactions of some of his colleagues. Hooker and Asa Gray were early supporters. Thomas H. Huxley was so charmed by the elegant simplicity of Darwin's argument that upon finishing the book he exclaimed, "How extremely stupid not to have thought of that!" Huxley was an instant convert, although he disagreed with Darwin on important points. But Darwin was sorry to learn that his old mentors, Adam Sedgwick and John S. Henslow, rejected natural selection; as clergymen, both were uncomfortable with the idea that life could evolve without the guiding hand of a creator.

The biggest disappointment was the reaction of Charles Lyell. The eminent geologist had been an important influence on Darwin and had later encouraged him to pursue and publish his theory. Darwin knew that an endorsement from Lyell—who was esteemed in social and political as well as scientific circles—would go far toward winning acceptance for the *Origin.* Yet Lyell's enthusiasm was subdued. He was a cautious man who valued his social position and his friendship with the royal family; he excelled at wrapping his own advanced ideas in careful language that would not offend conservative readers. Although he privately agreed with Darwin about evolution and natural selection, he never offered the wholehearted public support for which Darwin had hoped.

Darwin later adopted Lyell's public-relations tactics and used language that was designed to reassure the skittish reader. A significant example occurred in the second edition of the *Origin,* in which Darwin changed the final sentence to say that life had been "originally breathed by the Creator into a few forms or into one." Darwin added "by the Creator" to remind readers that natural selection did not necessarily banish God from the universe.

Yet in his chapter on "The Struggle for Existence," Darwin outlined the Malthusian doctrine that nature produces more organisms than can possibly survive as evidence that nature was often far from benevolent. He listed examples: songbirds that emerge from their eggs only to perish as nestlings, and seeds that never sprout. Elsewhere, he cited aspects of natural history that seemed too gruesome to be the work of a kindly God, such as the wasps that lay their eggs inside the bodies of living moth larvae, which are slowly devoured by the hatching wasps. Once Darwin burst out in a letter to Hooker, "What a book a Devil's Chaplain might write on the clumsy, wasteful, blundering low & horridly cruel works of nature!"

"Devil's Chaplain"—someone who preaches on behalf of the Devil, or against God—was a phrase Darwin remembered from his Cambridge years, when it had been applied to Robert Taylor, a renegade clergyman who had turned against Christianity. For his speeches denouncing the organized church, Taylor had been imprisoned as a threat to society. Darwin, despite his private agnosticism, did not set out to make an enemy of the church. Yet after the *Origin* was published, he was regarded by some people as a new "Devil's Chaplain."

Darwin numbered a good many devout Christians, and even some members of the clergy, among his supporters. Charles Kingsley, a well-known minister and author who saw no conflict between evolution and God, wrote to Darwin that it was just as noble to think that God had created "primal forms capable of self development" as to think that God had personally created every form. That view was shared by the prominent American preacher Henry Ward Beecher, who said, "I regard evolution as being the discovery of the Divine method in creation." Most of the clergy, however, were offended by the *Origin*. Evolution, they said, denied the biblical account of creation, and once people began doubting the Bible, where would they stop? Talk of evolution threatened the moral authority of the church, which was a political as well as a spiritual force. In the eyes of many, the spread of such ideas was dangerous, for it could destroy the social order.

No churchman attacked evolution more wittily than Samuel Wilberforce, the bishop of Oxford. Nicknamed "Soapy Sam" for his smooth talk and his slipperiness as a debater, Wilberforce was one of the lead players in a Darwinian drama that caused a sensation in June 1860. At the annual meeting of the British Association for the Advancement of Science, held at Oxford University, Wilberforce was scheduled to speak against Darwin and evolution. Darwin did not attend, but

A caricature of Samuel Wilberforce, bishop of Oxford and a prominent critic of Darwin's ideas.

his lieutenants Huxley and Hooker were on hand, ready to defend the theory. More than 700 people crowded into the lecture room, sensing that the debate could become lively.

Wilberforce spoke fluently, although he seemed to have little grasp of the scientific issues. His speech was directed at the emotions rather than the intellect. At one point he described how distressed he would be if it were proved to him that he had an "ape" in his family tree. The exact words of his next remark are lost, but many accounts of the meeting survive, and all agree that Wilberforce turned to Huxley and asked if it was on his grandfather's or his grandmother's side that Huxley claimed to be descended from an ape—a remark that was probably intended as a good-natured joke rather than a vicious insult.

Called upon by the audience to respond, Huxley replied that he would rather have an ape for a grandfather than an intelligent, influential man who used his great gifts for "the mere purpose of introducing ridicule into a grave scientific discussion." The room erupted into an excited babble. One lady was so overcome that she fainted.

The uproar caused by Huxley's retort had not died down when a gray-haired man stood up in the audience, holding a huge Bible over his head. It was Admiral Robert FitzRoy, who had been captain of the *Beagle* on Darwin's voyage. Darwin and FitzRoy, who had argued about slavery and the Bible, had drifted apart over the previous 30 years. FitzRoy had become a strict creationist who believed in the literal truth of the Bible. Now, declaring that the *Origin* had caused him "acutest pain," he urged his listeners to dismiss Darwin's ideas, but the crowd shouted him down and called for the next speaker. (FitzRoy, prone to fits of melancholy, came to a sad end; he slit his throat a few years after the Oxford debate.)

The next speaker at the debate was Hooker. In a measured and impressive speech, Hooker demonstrated to the audience that Wilberforce had not read the *Origin* and was

Thomas Henry Huxley, "Darwin's bulldog," lecturing on the skull of the gorilla. Huxley was one of Darwin's most earnest defenders.

ignorant of science. The bishop, Hooker exulted in a letter to Darwin, "had not one word to say in reply & the meeting was *dissolved forthwith* leaving you master of the field after 4 hours battle." But although Hooker had delivered the evolutionists' argument, it was Huxley's snappy exchange with the bishop that people remembered. The incident helped earn the nickname "Darwin's bulldog" for the tough, tenacious Huxley, who was always ready to go into battle for Darwin and evolution.

The bishop's jibe had struck at the heart of the most

The elderly Darwin appears as a monkey in a cartoon. For many people, the most disagreeable aspect of Darwinism was the idea that humans are part of the natural world, closely related to monkeys and apes.

disturbing aspect of Darwin's theory: the status of human beings. If species had evolved, how had humankind originated? Darwin's own views on the matter are clear. His notes and private correspondence show that he realized that all life, including humans, had evolved from a common ancestor, and that he recognized apes and monkeys as humankind's closest relatives. He did not, however, try to drive home this radical notion in the *Origin*. There he was prudently cautious on the subject of human evolution, predicting only that in the future, as evolutionary research continues, "Light will be thrown on the origin of man and his history." Still, Darwin's views on humankind's descent from the animal world could easily be read between the lines of the *Origin,* and scientists began debating the similarities and differences between people and apes. The attitude of pious and proper Victorians toward such speculations was summed up by the wife of the bishop of Worcester, who is said to have remarked, "Descended from the apes! My dear, let us hope that it is not true, but if it is, let us hope that it will not become generally known."

In the years after the publication of the *Origin,* a number of authors, including Lyell and Wallace, introduced the question of human evolution into their books. Huxley was particularly earnest in pursuing the subject. In 1863 he published *Evidence as to Man's Place in Nature,* in which, after showing that human beings are structurally related to gorillas and chimpanzees, he firmly placed *Homo sapiens* in the animal kingdom.

Even for some evolutionists, though, the inclusion of humans in the animal world was hard to swallow. Many, including Alfred Russel Wallace, believed that although humans had acquired their physical form through evolution and natural selection, their unique qualities of mind and soul were given to them by spiritual forces.

For the most part, Darwin was out of the public eye during the furor over evolution, although he followed its progress with keen attention and kept in close touch with his colleagues. Before long, the term "Darwinism" was being used to sum up Darwin's ideas, particularly the evolution of species, natural selection as the primary mechanism of evolution, the descent of all life from a common ancestor, and gradualism, the idea that evolution had happened slowly and gradually, not in sudden jumps. England's best-known Darwinists—aside from Darwin himself—were

text continues on page 99

During his lifetime, Darwin encountered much opposition. Most of it was on religious grounds; however, he also faced some objections from fellow scientists who believed that they had found flaws in his theories.

One objection ran this way: Darwin's evolutionary theory insists on a slow, gradual process of transformation from one species into another. But there are no fossils of the intermediate forms that should exist between the old and new species. Darwin knew very well that the fossil record was incomplete. He hoped that as paleontological research proceeded, new fossil finds would document the history of intermediate forms.

Darwin's expectations about future fossil finds were spectacularly rewarded in 1861, when a remarkable fossil came to light in Germany. Dubbed *Archaeopteryx,* it was a creature with the feathered wings of a bird and the teeth, spine, and tail of a lizard—a creature somewhere between a reptile and a bird, exactly the sort of thing Darwin had predicted. "The fossil bird," Darwin exulted, "is a grand case for me." Later, other intermediate forms turned up in the fossil record: additional links between reptiles and birds; an entire class of creatures that paleontologists call therapsids, or mammal-like reptiles, which bridge the gap between reptiles and mammals; and several complete sets of stages in the evolution of horses and other modern species.

At the same time, modern paleontologists have determined that the process of change was not always as slow and steady as Darwin believed. New forms sometimes appeared with relative abruptness; modification can apparently be rapid as well as slow. Biologists and paleontologists are working toward an understanding of these sudden jumps in the history of life. But Darwin was right in thinking that future fossil finds would support his belief in the existence of intermediate forms.

Another objection, and one that remained a problem throughout Darwin's life, involved time. Geology had opened up enormous vistas of "deep time," a history of the earth stretching back into aeons past. This concept of geological time was crucial to evolutionary thought. Darwin believed

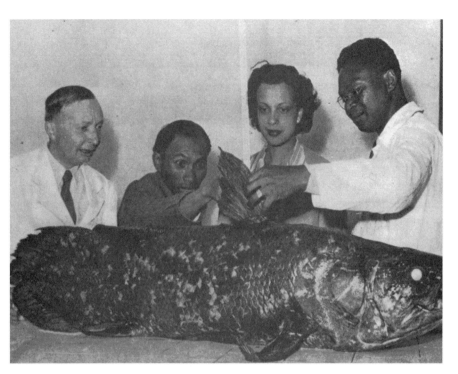

The coelacanth is a fish that scientists believed had been extinct for 60 or 70 million years—until a live one was captured in 1938 off the coast of Madagascar. Such "living fossils" prove Darwin's point that the fossil record is incomplete and only partially understood.

that all evolution came about through the slow accumulation of tiny, all-but-invisible modifications—a process that took ages upon ages. He agreed with geologist Charles Lyell that the earth was hundreds of millions of years old. In 1859, Darwin calculated that 300 million years had passed since the age of the dinosaurs.

But in 1862 a prominent physicist named Sir William Thomson, later Lord Kelvin, announced that he had determined the age of the planet using physics. Kelvin argued that the earth could not have been illuminated by the sun for the enormous lengths of time suggested by Lyell and Darwin. If the sun had existed for much longer than that, it would have run out of fuel and continued from previous page

ceased to provide heat and light. Using his calculations of the sun's age and of the rate at which the earth's temperature had cooled since its original molten state, Kelvin estimated the earth's age at about 100 million years. Others set the planet's age as low as 24 million years. But even Kelvin's estimate did not allow enough time for evolution to have occurred in the way Darwin had described.

Darwin felt certain that Kelvin was wrong about the earth's age, but he did not know how to prove it, and he admitted that Kelvin's was the most serious objection that his theory faced. The problem was not solved until after Darwin's death, when atomic energy and radioactivity were discovered. Atomic energy powers the sun, allowing it to last many times longer than Kelvin's 100 million years. In addition, radioactive elements inside the planet create heat, which means that the earth has cooled much more slowly than earlier physicists thought.

The earth is much older than Kelvin thought. Indeed, it is much older than *Darwin* thought: Current estimates put the planet's age at 4.5 billion years. Charles Darwin would probably respond to this news with a pleased, "All the more time for natural selection."

Huxley and Hooker. Darwinism's chief defender in the United States was botanist Asa Gray of Harvard University; its main attacker was zoologist Louis Agassiz (1807–73), also of Harvard. In Germany, Darwinism found a champion in Ernst Haeckel (1834–1919), a zoologist and anatomist who enthusiastically popularized evolution to the masses in speeches and articles. Through the efforts of these scientists, Darwin's ideas gradually came to be less controversial and more widely accepted. In the 20 years after the publication of the *Origin*, the popular image of Darwin changed from that of a dangerous but respectable troublemaker into that of a saintly scientist.

Meanwhile, Darwin continued to work as hard as he could. One task that kept him busy was preparing new editions of the *Origin*, which he revised five times between 1860 and 1872, adding new evidence and responding to criticisms. He also had to deal with a flood of letters from all over the world and with visitors who came to Down House hoping for a glimpse of the great man. Despite these distractions, Darwin managed to write 10 books after the *Origin*, several of them quite long. These works were detailed examinations of various aspects of evolution; they added to and expanded the ideas he had put forth in the *Origin*.

One line of work involved plants, with which Darwin had become increasingly fascinated, perhaps as a result of his association with the botanists Hooker and Gray. In 1862 he published *On the Various Contrivances by which Orchids are Fertilised by Insects,* in which he showed that the elaborate shapes and colors of orchid blossoms had evolved to attract the insects that pollinated the plants. The following year Darwin had a greenhouse built at Down. He spent many hours there studying and experimenting with plants; he was especially interested in insect-eating plants, such as the Venus flytrap, and in ivy and other climbing plants. His later plant books were *The Movements and Habits of Climbing*

Plants (1865), Insectivorous Plants (1875), The Effects of Cross and Self-Fertilisation in the Vegetable Kingdom (1876), The Different Forms of Flowers on Plants of the Same Species (1877), and finally The Power of Movement in Plants (1880), written with his son Francis.

In other works, Darwin explored in greater detail some of the topics he had touched on in the Origin. The two-volume Variation of Animals and Plants under Domestication (1868) covered domestic breeding at length, using material Darwin had prepared for the "big book" on species that he had abandoned to write the Origin. In Variation, Darwin introduced a theory that was criticized by Hooker, Huxley, and other supporters. He called it pangenesis, and it was his attempt to explain how parents transmit their characteristics to their offspring. Darwin believed that particles within the parents' bodies recorded their characteristics. This part of the pangenesis theory was correct; today those particles are called genes. Darwin was completely wrong, however, in believing that traits acquired during an organism's lifetime could be passed on to its children. This notion had been held by others before Darwin, notably by the French evolutionist Lamarck, but it has been discredited: acquired characteristics are not inherited. A bodybuilder can develop enormous muscles, but the bodybuilder's babies will not be born with bulging biceps.

In 1871 Darwin set out his views on the subject of human origins in The Descent of Man and Selection in Relation to Sex, which was really two books in one. In the first part, Darwin argued that humans had evolved from distant, ape-like ancestors, not, as many people mistakenly believed, from existing monkeys or apes. In the second part, Darwin set forth his theory that sexual selection, or the competition for mates, was a contributing factor in evolution. Darwin reasoned that some characteristics—such as the large, flamboyant tails of peacocks—do not help their owners obtain food or escape predators; they evolved because they helped

In a photograph taken a year before his death, Darwin appears as a weary, time-worn sage. "When I am obliged to give up observation and experiment," he said, "I shall die."

attract mates. Some human characteristics such as large but-tocks and fat lips, he suggested, might have evolved for the same reason. Darwin discussed human origins again in *The Expression of Emotions in Man and Animals* (1872), in which he described the evolution of smiles, frowns, and other forms of behavior—a subject that had interested him ever since he had watched his firstborn child smiling and crying in his crib.

Darwin's last book dealt with a humble subject—the earthworm, which, through slow and steady action, had created the earth's layer of soil. Like the power of natural selection itself, the earthworm was everywhere present, patiently, invisibly, and silently working to reshape the world. *The Formation of Vegetable Mould through the Action of Worms* (1881) reaffirmed Darwin's belief in gradualism, the accumulation of slow, tiny changes.

Throughout these years, Darwin watched with pride as his children grew up. Although he never pressured them to become scientists, he was happy when several sons chose scientific work. George became an astronomer and a professor at Cambridge University. Francis became a Cambridge botanist; he also edited his father's letters and the autobiographical essay Darwin wrote for his descendants. Horace, who had invented a device called a wormstone to help his father measure the rate at which worms formed new soil, founded a company to manufacture scientific instruments.

Darwin suffered a period of severe ill health in the mid-1860s. Afterward, his health improved somewhat, although as time went on he tired more and more easily. As he moved into old age, he had the satisfaction of knowing that he had done important scientific work to the best of his ability, and that his ideas had had a lasting effect upon the world. He dreaded the thought of going blind or of becoming so feeble that he could no longer work. "When I am obliged to give up observation and experiment, I shall die," he said.

In early 1882, Darwin had several minor heart attacks. A more serious attack followed, and Darwin died of cardiac disease on the afternoon of April 19 in his bed at Down House. A story began to circulate that on his deathbed Darwin had renounced evolution and declared himself a Christian, but that tale, like many stories about Darwin, was only a legend. Darwin's real deathbed statement was his calm remark to Emma on April 18: "I am not in the least afraid to die."

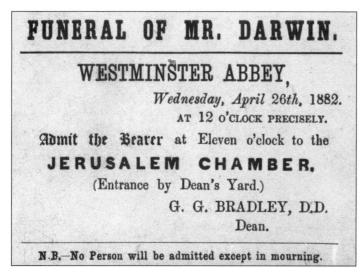

FUNERAL OF MR. DARWIN.

WESTMINSTER ABBEY,

Wednesday, April 26th, 1882.

AT 12 O'CLOCK PRECISELY.

Admit the Bearer at Eleven o'clock to the

JERUSALEM CHAMBER,

(Entrance by Dean's Yard.)

G. G. BRADLEY, D.D.
Dean.

N.B.—No Person will be admitted except in mourning.

Darwin's state funeral was a prestigious public occasion; admission was by ticket only.

Darwin had expected to be buried in the village where he had lived for so many years, but his scientific friends persuaded the family that Darwin deserved a greater honor. Such was his fame that neither bishops nor government ministers objected when a press campaign and political pressure from the Darwinists called for a state burial in Westminster Abbey, the London church where England's heroes were laid to rest. Darwin was buried there on April 26. Wallace, Huxley, Hooker, and the American ambassador helped carry his casket, and a throng of friends, colleagues, and stately public figures looked on while Darwin, who had once been reviled as the enemy of all that was sacred, was solemnly interred in the heart of the Anglican Church. Darwin, who possessed a keen sense of irony, would have enjoyed the spectacle.

OPINIONS

OF

MEN OF LIGHT & LEADING

And of the TIMES Newspaper, &c.,

ON

THE DARWIN CRAZE.

"A Gospel of Dirt."—Thomas Carlyle.

"I venture to think that no system of Philosophy that has ever been taught on earth lies under such a weight of antecedent improbability."
THE DUKE OF ARGYLL, in the *Contemporary Review*.

"The subtle sophistries of his (Huxley's) school are doing infinitely more mischief than the outspoken blasphemy of Bradlaugh."
J. M. WINN, M.D., M.R.C.P.

"The Science of those of his books which have made his chief title to fame, the "Origin of Species," and still more the "Descent of Man," is not Science, but a mass of assertions and absolutely gratuitous hypotheses, often evidently fallacious. This kind of publication and these theories are a bad example, which a body that respects itself cannot encourage."—LES MONDES.

(Darwin having been refused membership, as a correspondant, with the French Academy of Sciences, on the ground of the unscientific character of his books.)

BY

THE REV. F. O. MORRIS, B.A.,

Rector of Nunburnholme, Yorkshire,

AUTHOR OF "A HISTORY OF BRITISH BIRDS,"

Dedicated by permission to Her Most Gracious Majesty the Queen.

LONDON: W. S. PARTRIDGE & CO., PATERNOSTER ROW.

PRICE ONE PENNY.

An anti-Darwin publication from 1885. Thomas Carlyle, the historian whom Darwin had met decades earlier at Charles Babbage's parties, is quoted as calling Darwinism "A Gospel of Dirt."

CHAPTER

6

Darwin's Legacy

Thomas H. Huxley, "Darwin's bulldog," summed up his friend's achievement this way:

> None have fought better, and none have been more fortunate than Charles Darwin. He found a great truth, trodden underfoot, reviled by bigots, and ridiculed by all the world; he lived long enough to see it, chiefly by his own efforts, irrefragably established in science, inseparably incorporated with the common thoughts of men. . . . What shall a man desire more than this?

Darwin's "great truth," the evolution of life, has indeed become a key part of both science and common thought. But the path to acceptance was not always smooth, and controversy continues to swirl around Darwinism today. Darwin knew that new ideas in science often meet strong resistance, as people stubbornly cling to familiar beliefs. He wrote to a clergyman friend about the opposition to the *Origin of Species,* "By far the greater part of the opposition is just the same as that made when the sun was first said to stand still and the earth to go round." Darwin believed that his ideas, like those of Copernicus, who revolutionized astronomy in the early 16th century by proving that the earth revolves around the sun, would eventually prevail. One barrier to full understanding of Darwin's views is the fact that his basic idea has been applied in ways that go far beyond the realm of biology. The work of the philosopher Herbert Spencer (1820–1903) gave rise to a concept called Social Darwinism. Spencer was an early supporter of Darwinism. He coined the phrase "survival of the fittest" as a capsule description of natural selection, and Darwin adopted it in the fifth edition of the *Origin* (1869) and in *The Descent of Man* (1871). Spencer went on to apply the concept of the survival of the fittest to human society, suggesting that the suffering poor were being "eliminated" by natural selection because they were "unfit."

Others seized upon this idea; its most fervent supporters were American industrial millionaires, who believed that their great wealth proved that they were the "fittest" and who welcomed the vision of a world shaped by cutthroat competition and callous disregard for those who were less successful. Darwin, too, believed that the forces of evolution applied to human societies—for example, aboriginal cultures like the Tierra del Fuegians were being driven into extinction because they could not compete with the more powerful Western culture. But although Darwin felt that the moral sense of human beings was a product of evolution rather than a divine gift, he never denied that people possess a moral responsibility toward one another. Nonetheless, extreme versions of Social Darwinism have been used to justify racist atrocities, such as the extermination of Jews and other minorities held to be "unfit" by the Nazis, who believed themselves to be "racially superior."

Another area of confusion surrounds the concept of "progress." Evolution has often been confused with progress—that is, with movement in a particular direction. Theories of evolution before Darwin, such as that of Lamarck, saw evolution as a progression upward from "lower" to "higher" forms of life. This progressive view enabled many people to accept evolution, especially the evolution of human beings; they did not particularly like the idea that they had evolved from apes, but at least they could take comfort in the thought that their great-great-grandchildren would be superior beings. Many of the clergy who embraced Darwinism did so in the belief that evolution equalled progress away from humankind's brute beginnings toward a more highly evolved spiritual state.

Stephen Jay Gould of Harvard University, an evolutionary biologist and a historian of Darwinism, has shown that Darwin himself was not consistent about the difference between evolution and progress. Strictly speaking, Darwin's

"The world has been different ever since Darwin," says Stephen Jay Gould, one of the foremost modern evolutionary biologists. Gould's books and articles have introduced many nonscientists to Darwin and to evolutionary science.

theory of natural selection says that organisms adapt to local changes in their environments; it makes no claims for adaptation in any particular direction, for overall progress or "improvement." Darwin wrote to an American paleontologist named Alpheus Hyatt in 1872, "After long reflection, I cannot avoid the conviction that no innate tendency to progressive development exists." Yet Darwin lived in an era and a society that was bursting with pride in its industrial, imperial, and social "progress," and he could not completely shake off the pervasive notion that change meant betterment. Some of his statements can therefore be taken as claims that evolution is progressive, that organisms become not just different but better. As a result, Darwin has been cited as an authority both by those who see evolution as progress and by those who see it as change without an overall direction. The majority of scientists today favor the latter view: Evolution means change, but it does not necessarily mean progress toward a "higher" state.

Religion has provided the most stubborn opposition to Darwinism. The conflict between evolution and religion did not end with the notorious Oxford debate in 1860. For years, Darwin's ideas were rejected by those who felt that they violated prevailing religious beliefs. This feeling was particularly strong in the Christian fundamentalist movement that arose in the United States in the early years of the 20th century. The word "fundamentalist" was coined by a Baptist editor who used it to refer approvingly to those who did battle for the "great fundamentals" of traditional Christianity. One of those fundamental beliefs was that the Bible taught scientific truths. Although a few early fundamentalist leaders accepted evolution and found that it was compatible with their belief in God, by the 1920s fundamentalism had mounted a biblical crusade against Darwinism.

The issue went to the courts in 1925 in Tennessee, when a public high school teacher named John T. Scopes was put on trial for teaching human evolution after a new state law forbade such teaching in public schools. Scopes deliberately broke the law in order to call national attention to it; the American Civil Liberties Union charged that the law violated his right to free speech.

The Scopes trial—or the Monkey Trial, as some called it, parodying Darwin's views on human origins—was a landmark in scientific history. It pitted prosecutor William Jennings Bryan, a well-known political orator and a sophisticated, well-read fundamentalist, against Clarence Darrow, a radical lawyer who took on Scopes's defense. Another key character was H. L. Mencken, a young reporter who captured the events of the trial in witty stories, portraying Bryan as a pompous windbag and Darrow as a sharp-witted freethinker. In a 1960 movie about the trial, *Inherit the Wind,* Fredric March played the conservative prosecutor, Spencer Tracy played the liberal defense lawyer, and Gene Kelly played the reporter.

To no one's surprise, Scopes lost the trial. He admitted that he had broken the law, and he was convicted and fined

The 1925 Scopes case put evolution on trial in Tennessee.

$100, although the conviction was later overturned because of a legal technicality. In the larger sense, though, the trial had been a battle of ideas, and there the victory was not so clear. Bryan had claimed that the Bible was the word of God and was not subject to human "interpretation," but Darrow's cross-examination forced Bryan to admit that he did "interpret" the Bible—for example, Bryan admitted that he did not believe that the sun revolves around the earth, even though passages in the Bible seem to suggest that it does. Darrow then pointed out that if one interpretation could be made, thousands could be made. Bryan and his supporters emerged from the fray looking like narrow-minded, illogical bigots, and to some people evolution appeared more respectable than ever. The Tennessee law remained on the books until 1967, but it was not enforced. Scientists congratulated themselves that the forces of logic and intellectual liberty had won the day.

Such congratulations were premature. Fundamentalist opposition to Darwinism continues, and since the 1970s groups of fundamentalists—also called creationists because of their conviction that life was miraculously created—have been active in a number of school systems, promoting the teaching of what they call "creation science" as an alternative to evolutionary biology. Creation science attempts to explain the history of the earth and of life in a way that does not conflict with the Book of Genesis. The courts have consistently ruled that creation science is religion, not science, and therefore is not to be taught in public classrooms.

The debate between creationists and evolutionists is a heated one, with deeply felt passions on both sides. Creationists feel that the theory of evolution attacks the very heart of their spiritual belief, and they object to their children being taught something that conflicts with their religious doctrines. On the other hand, evolutionists maintain that the heart of the issue lies in the differences between *theory, fact,* and *belief.* Evolution is a theory, a statement that explains observable phenomena. It is supported by a vast number of facts: the geological record, the structural relationships among species, variations among both domestic and wild species of plants and animals, and more. Like any theory, it is flexible. It may be—and has been—modified to account for new facts as they arise. The biblical story of creation, on the other hand, is not supported by facts; instead, it is contradicted by many well-known facts. It cannot be the basis for a scientific theory, although it may form the grounds for belief, or faith, which does not demand evidence.

In his 1991 book *Darwin on Trial,* Philip E. Johnson, a professor of law at the University of California at Berkeley, makes a useful distinction. He points out that some Christian fundamentalists, whom he calls "creation-scientists," insist upon the literal truth of the Bible's account of creation in six days. Other creationists accept that the earth is billions of years old and that life has evolved, but they believe that this process has been guided by God. Johnson, who attempts to show that the evolutionists are as biased toward their own views as the creationists are toward theirs, argues that Darwinism rules out God altogether. Johnson errs here, however, for in fact, Darwinism simply explains life as a natural process, one that does not require supernatural or divine intervention. It does not say that God does not exist; it merely says that God is not a *necessary* part of the history of life. As far as evolutionary science is concerned, there may or may not be a God. To creationists, however, it is an article of faith that life cannot be explained without a God. Divine creation forms the bedrock of their moral systems. The creation-scientists, who insist that the Book of Genesis is literally true, are especially militant in their belief that the teaching of evolutionary science is an attack on God. The clash of ideas between science and religion is thus likely to continue.

text continues on page 114

One aspect of evolution that Darwin never understood to his satisfaction was heredity—the mechanism by which characteristics are passed from an organism to its offspring. Heredity certainly existed, but how? Ironically, the key to understanding heredity was found during Darwin's lifetime but never came to his attention. It lay in the works of an obscure Austrian monk and naturalist named Gregor Mendel (1822–84).

For 15 years, beginning in 1850, Mendel carried out thousands of experiments in the breeding of plant hybrids, or crosses between varieties. He used two types of pea plants: tall and short. He found that if he crossed a tall plant with a short one, all of their offspring were tall. When he crossed two of these second-generation offspring, however, he produced a third generation that contained one short plant for every three tall plants.

At the time, the prevailing view of heredity held that the traits of parents were equally mixed in their offspring. This gave rise to the so-called paintpot problem of evolution, posed in 1867 by a Scottish engineer named Henry Fleeming Jenkin (1853–85). Jenkin said that variations in individuals could not be the basis of new species because these variations would soon be lost or swamped, bred back into the main population, just as a single drop of black paint would disappear if stirred into a pot of white paint.

By 1867, when Jenkin made his paintpot argument against natural selection, Mendel had observed thousands of experiments that proved that parental characteristics were not "blended" in offspring. If inheritance were blended, as Jenkin and others believed, then Mendel's crosses of tall and short pea plants would have produced medium plants. Instead, all of the plants produced in successive generations were either tall or short, with tall predominating. Inheritance, then, was not blended; traits were inherited in their entirety. The way these traits were distributed among offspring depended upon factors that Mendel called dominance and recessiveness. Dominant traits (tallness, in the case of Mendel's pea plants) appeared in all first-generation offspring and three-fourths of second-generation offspring.

It is not clear whether Mendel understood the full significance of his dis-

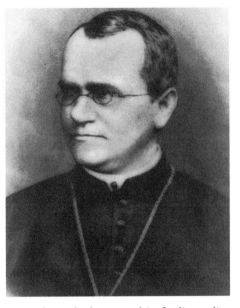

Gregor Mendel, the obscure Austrian monk whose experiments with pea plants held the key to the problem of heredity.

covery. In 1866 he published his findings in an article in a small local journal of natural history; that same year, he was made head of his monastery and gave up his plant experiments for administrative duties. Upon his death in 1884, all of his notes and papers were discarded. Mendel's article found its way to a few scientists, but they took little interest in it, partly because Mendel was so obscure and partly because his findings disagreed with the widely held notion of blended inheritance.

Around 1900, however, several scientists working on the problem of heredity recognized the significance of Mendel's paper and followed his approach in studying inheritance. Soon after, the new science of cellular biology allowed researchers to discover that heredity is governed by special cells that carry genes, or units of heredity, from parents to offspring. In 1953, scientists James Watson and Francis Crick revealed that genetic material consists of molecules of deoxyribose nucleic acid (DNA). The study of heredity had made enormous leaps forward in the century since Gregor Mendel planted his first pea plants, but it was his patient experiments that had paved the way for the new science of molecular genetics.

text continued from page 111

Darwinism has faced scientific obstacles as well as religious opposition. One of the biggest obstacles, as Darwin knew, was the lack of knowledge about how traits are transmitted from parents to offspring. Gregor Mendel had begun to solve that problem by experimenting with plant breeding in the 1850s and 1860s, but his work did not become generally known until the beginning of the 20th century, when the laws of inheritance began to be formulated. Around the same time, great advances were made in the study of cellular biology, and soon scientists had determined that the inheritance of characteristics was linked to certain cells. The science of genetics—the study of heredity and variation in organisms and populations—was born. In the 1960s came the discovery of deoxyribose nucleic acid, or DNA, and the birth of the modern science of molecular genetics. DNA, which consists of strands of phosphates and sugars bonded together in long molecules, encodes the genetic information that is the basis for life. Through DNA, genetic information from parent organisms is transmitted to and combined in their offspring.

During Darwin's lifetime and for some years afterward, evolution was accepted far more readily than natural selection. There was convincing evidence that species had evolved, but the mechanism of evolution was not so obvious. During the final decades of the 19th century and the early years of the 20th, scientists advanced a number of ideas about evolution that ignored or downplayed natural selection as a mechanism. For a time it was thought that evolution was caused by mutations—sudden, drastic changes in organisms' structures—rather than by the slow accumulation of small changes that Darwin had proposed. Then, in the 1920s and 1930s, natural selection came back into the picture when geneticists proved that small changes in a few organisms could lead to changes in large populations.

Around 1940, a group of scientists—including the Russian-American geneticist Theodosius Dobzhansky

(1900–75) and the biologist Julian Huxley (1887–1975), grandson of Thomas H. Huxley—brought Darwin's ideas about natural selection together with new studies in Mendelian genetics, paleontology, and other fields in what has been called the "New Synthesis" (a synthesis is a combination of elements), the "Synthetic Theory," or Neo-Darwinism (*neo* means new). One of the leading spokespeople for the New Synthesis has been biologist Ernst Mayr, who wrote about Darwin, "We turn to him again and again, because as a bold and intelligent thinker he raised some of the most profound questions about our origins that have ever been asked, and as a devoted and innovative scientist he provided brilliant, often world-shattering answers."

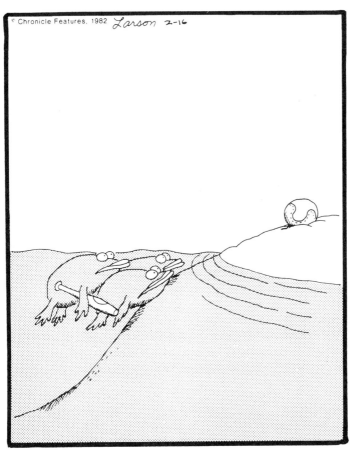

© Chronicle Features. 1982 *Larson* 2-16

Great moments in evolution.

The once-radical idea of evolution has permeated popular culture. Gary Larson's cartoon, for example, offers a whimsical answer to the question: If life originated in the oceans, as biologists believe, how and why did it spread to the land?

Today the fact of evolution is accepted by the vast majority of scientists. But evolutionary biology did not screech to a halt once the New Synthesis was reached. Since the 1940s, new areas of evolutionary science have been opened up for exploration. Scientists have come up with important new ideas about the rate at which evolutionary change occurs and the mechanisms that bring it about. They are debating the role of chance, luck, and random circumstance in evolution; they are questioning the importance of natural selection and proposing additional mechanisms of change; they are using new techniques from the genetic sciences to determine when species split off from other species; and they are studying new fossil finds to learn more about humankind's place in the natural world. Some biologists, led by Richard Dawkins in England and Edward O. Wilson in the United States, have explored the concept of sociobiology, which explains human and animal behavior in terms of evolution. Sociobiologists attempt to explain such characteristics as monogamy and self-sacrifice—for example, by showing how a bird that calls attention to a predator by uttering a warning cry to other birds may be preserving the genetic heritage of its close relatives, although the calling bird itself runs a greater risk of being caught and eaten by the predator. Meanwhile, as new theories of evolutionary biology are proposed and tested, historians of evolution are combing archives to piece together a more accurate picture of Darwin's thought.

All of these activities are an extension of Darwin's own constant experimentation and revision of his work. Darwin knew that science never stands still. One contributor's conclusions are the starting point for later investigators. Today's evolutionary explorers share Darwin's passion: the quality that his friend and colleague Alfred Russel Wallace called "his insatiable longing to discover the causes of the varied and complex phenomena presented by living things."

CHRONOLOGY

1809
Charles Darwin born at Shrewsbury, England, February 12

1817
Mother dies

1817–25
Attends Shrewsbury School

1825–27
Studies medicine at Edinburgh University, Scotland

1828–31
Attends Cambridge University, England

1831–36
Travels around world on survey ship *Beagle*

1837
Begins first notebook on changes in species

1838
Reads Thomas Malthus's *Essay on the Principle of Population*

1839
Marries Emma Wedgwood in January; son William born
in December; first period of severe illness

1839–43
Edits five volumes on zoology of *Beagle* voyage

1842
Moves to Down House, outside London

1842–46
Writes three volumes on geology of *Beagle* voyage

1844
Writes unpublished essay on evolution

1846–55
Studies and writes about barnacles

1848
Father dies; prolonged period of ill health

1851
Daughter Annie dies

1855
Begins writing major book about evolution

1858
Paper on Darwin's and Alfred Russel Wallace's theory of evolution is read at Linnean Society, London

1859
On the Origin of Species published

1860
Evolution debated at British Association meeting, Oxford

1863–65
Prolonged illness

1868
Variation under Domestication published

1870s
Five books on plants published

1871
Descent of Man published

1872
Expression of the Emotions published

1881
Book on earthworms published

1882
Dies at Down House, April 19; buried in Westminster Abbey

biology   The study of living organisms.

botany   The study of plants.

DNA   Deoxyribose nucleic acid, the material that makes up chromosomes, long molecules that carry genes, the units of heredity.

creationism   The belief that the world and all living things were created by God, as in the Judeo-Christian history recounted in the Bible. The term is usually used to refer to the strict, literal interpretation of the Bible followed by certain fundamentalists who claim that God's creation took six days and occurred only a few thousand years ago.

ecological niche   An organism's place in the ecosystem, or web of interactions among organisms and the environment. A niche is defined by where an organism lives, what it eats, what eats it, and so on.

endemic   Limited to a single place; found nowhere else.

extinction   The disappearance of all living members of a species or of a larger biological grouping such as a family or an order.

evolution   The process by which species change, or evolve, over time, with new species emerging from old ones. The theory of evolution is commonly credited to Darwin, who declared that all forms of life on earth, both living and extinct, are related to one another and are descended from the same ancestral forms. The fact that evolution has occurred is well established; the ways in which it takes place are still being studied.

fossil   Traces of ancient life preserved in the earth. Bones, eggs, leaves, shells, pollen, footprints, and other remains become fossilized when organic material is replaced by minerals over a long period of time.

gene   The fundamental unit of heredity that transfers traits from parents to offspring; genes are carried on chromosomes, which are strands of a material called deoxyribose nucleic acid (DNA).

genetics   The study of heredity and variation in organisms.

geology   The study of how the earth was formed, of the processes that have shaped the land, and of the materials of which the earth is made.

heredity   The transmission of characteristics from parents to offspring.

mutation   A random change in a gene. Mutations arise when cells copy DNA incorrectly; the genes may be improperly duplicated, or part of a chromosome may be omitted or reversed. Mutations are one source of variation among organisms.

naturalist   A student of natural history.

natural history   The study of the earth and of living things. Today natural history is generally divided into many specialized areas of study, including geology, zoology, botany, and paleontology.

natural selection   The term coined by Darwin to describe one of the principal means by which new species are created. Natural selection means that features that improve an organism's chances of survival will be passed on to future generations because the organism will be more likely to live long and reproduce. Features that work against an organism's survival are less likely to be passed on because the organism will have less chance to reproduce. The same principle applies to the deliberate breeding of animal variations and plant hybrids by farmers; this is called artificial selection.

paleontology   The study of past life forms, chiefly through fossils.

species   A population of organisms all of which can interbreed and produce fertile offspring.

subspecies   A group of organisms within a species that share one or more distinguishing features. Members of the subspecies can interbreed with the larger species but usually do not do so; they may be reproductively isolated by geography or some other factor. A variety is also a group of organisms within a species; often the term is used for a group that is less distinct from the main species than a subspecies would be.

sexual selection   Darwin's term for the process by which animals develop qualities that make them more successful in attracting mates; for example, when female birds choose mates with elaborate or colorful plumage, those traits are emphasized in the offspring, and characteristics such as the peacock's tail emerge. Sexual selection is a form of natural selection driven by reproductive patterns.

variety   A group of organisms within a species. Members of a variety are set apart from the main species by a trait or traits but can interbreed with the main species.

zoology   The study of animals.

Books by Charles Darwin

Appleman, Philip, ed. *Darwin.* 2nd ed. New York: Norton, 1979.
A selection of excerpts from Darwin's works.

Barrett, Paul, Peter Gautrey, Sandra Herbert, David Kohn, and
Sydney Smith, eds. *Charles Darwin's Notebooks, 1836–1844.*
Ithaca, N.Y.: Cornell University Press, 1987.

Burkhardt, Frederick, and Sydney Smith, eds. *The Correspondence
of Charles Darwin.* 7 vols. Cambridge: Cambridge University
Press, 1985–1991.

Darwin, Charles. *On the Origin of Species by Means of Natural
Selection.* New York: Avenel, 1979. Reprint of first (1859)
edition.

——. *On the Origin of Species.* New York: Random House,
1993.

——. *The Voyage of the Beagle.* Introduction by Walter
Sullivan. New York: New American Library, 1972. First published in 1839.

Darwin, Francis, ed. *The Autobiography of Charles Darwin and
Selected Letters.* 1892. Reprint, New York: Dover, 1958.
Reprint of 1892 edition.

Jastrow, Robert, ed. *The Essential Darwin.* Selections and com-
mentary by Kenneth Korey. Boston: Little, Brown, 1984.

Keynes, R. D., ed. *Charles Darwin's Beagle Diary.* Cambridge:
Cambridge University Press, 1988.

Leakey, Richard E., ed. *The Illustrated Origin of Species.* New
York: Hill and Wang, 1979. An abridged and illustrated ver-
sion that shows how modern scietists have interpreted the
Origin.

Darwin's Life and Work

Aaseng, Nathan. *Charles Darwin: Revolutionary Biologist.*
Minneapolis: Lerner, 1993.

Allan, Mea. *Darwin and His Flowers: The Key to Natural Selection.* New York: Taplinger, 1977.

Bowlby, John. *Charles Darwin: A New Life.* New York: Norton, 1990.

Bowler, Peter J. *Charles Darwin: The Man and His Influence.* Cambridge, Mass.: Blackwell, 1990.

Browne, Janet. *Charles Darwin: Voyaging.* New York: Knopf, 1995. Volume one of a biography.

Brackman, Arnold. *A Delicate Arrangement: The Strange Case of Charles Darwin and Alfred Russel Wallace.* New York: Times Books, 1980.

Clark, Ronald W. *The Survival of Charles Darwin: A Biography of a Man and an Idea.* New York: Avon, 1986.

Colp, Ralph, Jr. *To Be an Invalid: The Illness of Charles Darwin.* Chicago: University of Chicago Press, 1977.

Desmond, Adrian, and James Moore. *Darwin.* New York: Warner, 1991.

Gruber, Howard E. *Darwin on Man: A Psychological Study of Scientific Creativity.* 2nd ed. Chicago: University of Chicago Press, 1981.

Himmelfarb, Gertrude. *Darwin and the Darwinian Revolution.* New York: Norton, 1968.

Hull, David. *Darwin and His Critics: The Reception of Darwin's Theory of Evolution by the Scientific Community.* Chicago: University of Chicago Press, 1983.

Irvine, William. *Apes, Angels, and Victorians: The Story of Darwin, Huxley, and Evolution.* New York: McGraw-Hill, 1955.

Marks, Richard Lee. *Three Men of the Beagle.* New York: Knopf, 1991.

Milner, Richard. *Charles Darwin.* New York: Facts on File, 1993.

Moorehead, Alan. *Darwin and the Beagle.* New York: Harper & Row, 1969.

Nardo, Don. *Charles Darwin.* New York: Chelsea House, 1993.

Shapiro, Irwin. *Darwin and the Enchanted Isles.* New York: Coward, McCann and Geogehan, 1977.

Stevens, Lewell Robert. *Charles Darwin.* Boston: Twayne, 1978.

Ward, Peter. *The Adventure of Charles Darwin: A Story of the Beagle Voyage.* Cambridge: Cambridge University Press, 1986.

Darwinism and Evolution

Attenborough, David. *Discovering Life on Earth: A Natural History.* Boston: Little, Brown, 1981.

Bailey, Marilyn. *Evolution: Opposing Viewpoints.* San Diego: Greenhaven, 1990.

Berra, Tim M. *Evolution and the Myth of Creationism: A Basic Guide to the Facts in the Evolution Debate.* Stanford: Stanford University Press, 1990.

Bowler, Peter J. *Evolution: The History of an Idea.* Berkeley: University of California Press, 1984.

Eldredge, Niles, ed. *The Natural History Reader in Evolution.* New York: Columbia University Press, 1987.

Emory, Jerry. "Managing Another Galapagos Species—Man." *National Geographic,* January 1988, pp. 146–54.

Futuyma, Douglas. *Science on Trial: The Case for Evolution.* New York: Pantheon, 1983.

Gallant, Roy A. *Before the Sun Dies: The Story of Evolution.* New York: Macmillan, 1989.

Gould, Stephen Jay, ed. *The Book of Life.* New York: Norton, 1993.

———. *Ever Since Darwin: Reflections in Natural History.* New York: Norton, 1977.

———. "Evolution as Fact and Theory." In *Hen's Teeth and Horse's Toes: Further Reflections in Natural History.* New York: Norton, 1983.

———. "What Is a Species?" *Discover,* December 1992, p. 40.

Huxley, Julian. *The Wonderful World of Life.* Garden City, N.Y.: Doubleday, 1969.

Johnson, Phillip E. *Darwin on Trial.* Washington, D.C.: Regnery Gateway, 1991.

Levine, George L. *Darwin and the Novelists: Patterns of Science in Victorian Fiction.* Cambridge: Harvard University Press, 1988.

Lewin, Roger. *Human Evolution: An Illustrated Introduction.* New York: Freeman, 1984.

———. *Thread of Life.* Washington: Smithsonian Books, 1982.

Marshall, Kim. *The Story of Life: From the Big Bang to You.* New York: Holt, Rinehart and Winston, 1980.

Mayr, Ernst. *One Long Argument: Charles Darwin and the Genesis of Modern Evolutionary Thought.* Cambridge: Harvard University Press, 1991.

McGowen, Tom. *The Great Monkey Trial: Science versus Fundamentalism in America.* New York: Watts, 1990.

Miller, Jonathan and Borin van Loon. *Darwin for Beginners.* New York: Pantheon, 1982.

Milner, Richard. *The Encyclopedia of Evolution: Humanity's Search for Its Origins.* New York: Facts on File, 1990.

Montagu, Ashley, editor. *Science and Creationism.* New York: Oxford University Press, 1984.

Moore, James. *The Post-Darwinian Controversies: A Study of the Protestant Struggle to Come to Terms with Darwin, 1870–1900.* Cambridge: Cambridge University Press, 1979.

Nash, J. Madeleine. "How Did Life Begin?" *Time,* October 11, 1993, p. 68.

Numbers, Ronald L. *The Creationists.* New York: Knopf, 1992.

Peters, David. *From the Beginning: The Story of Human Evolution.* New York: Morrow, 1991.

Plage, Dieter and Mary. "A Century After Darwin's Death: Galapagos Wildlife Under Pressure." *National Geographic,* January 1988, pp. 122–45.

Raup, David M. *Extinction: Bad Genes or Bad Luck?* New York: Norton, 1991.

Ruse, Michael. *The Darwinian Revolution.* Chicago: University of Chicago Press, 1979.

Stanley, Steven M. *Extinction.* New York: Scientific American Books, 1987.

Weiner, Jonathan. *The Beak of the Finch: A Story of Evolution in Our Time.* New York: Knopf, 1994.

Wilson, Edward O. *The Diversity of Life.* Cambridge: Harvard University Press, 1992.

Rebecca Stefoff has written more than 50 books for young adults, specializing in geography and biography. Her previous books about scientific issues include *Extinction* and *Environmental Disasters*. Her lifelong interest in reading and collecting travel narratives is reflected in such titles as *Lewis and Clark, Magellan and the Discovery of the World Ocean, Marco Polo and the Medieval Travelers, Vasco da Gama and the Portuguese Explorers, The Viking Explorers,* and numerous books on China, Japan, Mongolia, the Middle East, and Latin America. Books on exploration include *Accidental Explorers, Women of the World,* and *Scientific Explorers.* Ms. Stefoff has served as editorial director of two Chelsea House series, *Places and Peoples of the World* and *Let's Discover Canada,* and as a geography consultant for the *Silver Burdett Countries* series. She earned her Ph.D. at the University of Pennsylvania and lives in Portland, Oregon.

Owen Gingerich is a senior astronomer at the Smithsonian Astrophysical Observatory and Professor of Astronomy and of the History of Science at Harvard University. He has served as vice president of the American Philosophical Society and as chairman of the U.S. National Committee of the International Astronomical Union. The author of more than 400 articles and reviews, Professor Gingerich is also the author of *The Great Copernicus Chase and Other Adventures in Astronomical History,* and *The Eye of Heaven: Ptolemy, Copernicus, Kepler.* The International Astronomical Union's Minor Planet Bureau has named Asteroid 2658 "Gingerich" in his honor.